WORLD OF HERBS

WORLD OF HERBS

RECIPES, REMEDIES
AND DECORATIVE IDEAS

Lesley Bremness

To J. Roger Lowe

First published by Ebury Press
an imprint of the Random House Group Limited
Random House
20 Vauxhall Bridge Road
London SW1V 2SA

Designed and typeset by Dorchester Typesetting
Printed and bound by Biddles Ltd, Guildford and King's Lynn

CONTENTS

INTRODUCTION

Herbs are plants which enhance our lives, as they serve and delight us. The closer we are to nature, the more plants we consider valuable and hence are considered to be herbs. To the early races and the aboriginal groups still close to nature, almost all plants were considered herbs as they were useful. The Cree Indians say the following when collecting medicinal plants: 'Oh great spirit of the heavens, we beg of you and Mother Earth with her great gifts, that this remedy will do good to those who suffer, we are very thankful.'

In the opening chapter of Genesis, verse 11, the Bible says: 'And God said "Let the earth bring forth grass, the herb yielding seed, and the fruit tree yielding fruit . . ." ' Here, 'herb' appears to include any plant that is neither grass nor a tree; a large range similar to those today classified as herbaceous. Indeed, the two words have the same root.

All the early civilizations valued a large number of herbs. Chinese, Indian, Assyrian and Egyptian cultures each had medical and mystical treatises about the healing and sacred properties of several hundred plants. There were many herbs used for flavouring food, beauty treatments, crafts and celebrations but less is written about these. The recognition of a large number of herbs continued through Greek and Roman societies to Europe and Charlemagne who, in 812 AD, ordered a set list of herbs to be grown on all the imperial farms in his empire.

In sixteenth-century Britain, a wide range of plants were still considered to be herbs, and were roughly divided into four groups. First were the pot herbs, those added to the cooking pot for bulk which included plants like carrots, onions and leeks. (The word 'vegetable' only came into its present meaning around 200 years ago.) Then there were 'sallet' herbs: those used to create a salad, historically a much more adventurous dish than present day efforts. The third group comprised the sweet herbs used as flavourings, probably the closest to the more recent meaning of the word herb. Several retained this in their names such as sweet cicely, sweet woodruff and sweet marjoram. Finally, there were 'simples'; single herbs used as medical treatments or mixed together to create 'compounds'.

What caused the dramatic reduction in the number of plants we call herbs so that by the early to mid-twentieth century the number was reduced to only a few seasoning herbs such as parsley, sage, rosemary, thyme, mint and chives? Part of the answer lies in the effect of science on western development in general and on our relationship with nature and useful plants in particular.

In the thirteenth century BC, there lived in Greece a healer who many felt was divinely inspired. His name was Asclepius and he was skilled in the use of herbs. He designed a healing system which by changing old thinking patterns could transform individuals. In this he seems to have understood and treated aspects of stress. Many miracles of healing were attributed to Asclepius and his three healing daughters: Hygieia, Iaso and Panacea. Eventually he was deified and healing temples sprang up across Greece.

The system of Asclepius was practised in Greece for several hundred years and there are temple remains at Cos, Athens and, the most famous, at Epidaurus. Some of his ideas continue today in therapy centres and health resorts.

The inspirational aspect of science is again represented in the work of philosopher and mathematician Pythagorus whose ideas on harmony, theorems of geometry and discoveries about the vibrations of sound were the result of meditation. In the sixth century BC, Pythagorus set up a university to teach the key to universal harmony, both natural and social. Herbs played an important part in the cleansing and restorative routine which preceded advanced learning. Poultices were the favourite method of applying herbs to create a longer, continuous contact with the plants. Herbs were also used in the special high energy food mixture created for his long sojourns alone for contemplation.

Scholarship flourished in Classical Greece in which the natural world was still considered man's dominant partner. The major contribution of Hippocrates (460–377 BC) was to place a scientific framework of diagnosis and treatment around western medicine. He was one of the Aesclepiadae, a group of physicians named after Aesclepius. From him the Hippocratic Oath, a code of conduct for the medical profession, is still honoured by doctors throughout the world. He tried to eliminate the idea of disease as being punishment from the gods and considered food, occupation and climate important factors in disease. He wrote 'Our natures are the physicians of our diseases', and that patients should help their bodies to heal themselves by diet and plant medicines.

Aristotle was one of the world's greatest scholars with interests ranging over the entire natural world including ethics and metaphysics. He championed accurate observation and disciplined theorizing. He organized biological science and wrote many plant descriptions. Philosophy, botany and healing were closely linked; it was a golden age for enquiring minds.

Perhaps the highpoint of herbal knowledge was reached around the time of Hypatia (370–415). The sum of human knowledge had been collected and translated at the famous university library in Alexandria. Hypatia was a child prodigy, tutored by the finest scholars of her day. She became famous for her knowledge in the fields of mathematics, astronomy and natural sciences and was eventually appointed head of the University of Alexandria and a government advisor. In her popular lectures, Hypatia tried to effect an intellectual reawakening of the concepts of the Greek deities, particularly the feminine Earth Mother because she could see that respect for the

Mother Goddess would return respect and power to women. But she was anathema to the Catholic Church and the Bishop of Alexandria despised her. He did not have the power to openly criticize her so he directed a group of fanatical monks to attack her. They viciously hacked her to pieces and burnt the remains.

This could be considered a pointer to the Dark Ages to come. Whereas steps had been taken to rise above the superstitions and ignorance of the past by free-thinking scholars, they were now forbidden to think outside the boundaries imposed by the Catholic Church. The result of this intellectual stifling had such a crippling effect on thinkers and scientists that later, when they were free from these restrictions, the backlash of their treatment resulted in a condemnation of all metaphysical ideas. Ripples still affect objective judgement of the natural sciences, inspirational thought and complementary medicine today.

Through the Dark Ages there was some contact with Arab cultures which had preserved the Greek heritage and made advances in medicine. The court physician, Avicenna (980–1037), an outstanding student of all the natural sciences of his day: philosophy, astronomy, logic, geometry, metaphysics as well as medicine, produced his 'Canon of Medicine' which became a standard university textbook for 600 years.

There was the occasional spark of light during Europe's Dark Ages. One was the writing of Hildegarde of Bingen, an abbess, scientist, musician, herbal healer, prophetess and visionary. In her two works, Physica and Causa et Cure, she was probably the first to use common names along with Latin names for herbs.

But early in the fifteenth century, the general economy of Europe had been weakened by the Black Death; universities were in decline and the Church was disintegrating. Apart from isolated examples of free thinking, dogma dominated religion, philosophy, medicine and many other branches of learning, including herbalism.

By good fortune, several ideas matured concurrently. The first area of fresh thinking in Europe came in the Renaissance of Italy where artists rediscovered classical Greek and Latin thinking and their human, as opposed to divine, centred universe. The visual arts and their craftsmen rose in social esteem and artists became people of wide cultural interests, exemplified by Leonardo Da Vinci.

At the same time, in a mining area of southern Germany, practical mathematics was being used to develop skills in metallurgy. Along the trade route from this area to the weaving centres of Flanders, these skills were used to create the alloy metals suitable for making the replaceable bits of type for the printing press of Gütenberg. Once developed, the press spread rapidly along the trade routes. Herbals were among the first books published and there was an explosion of learning from this newly available information.

World travel routes were being discovered. The desire for spices introduced from the Orient and the lucrative business involved led to a search for new sources of these products and new trade routes by the Spanish and Portuguese. The resulting world exploration brought the 'discovery' of the Americas and Australia. On the return currents, new plants were introduced from the New

World and the Far East along with their herbal uses.

The new philosophy of the seventeenth century propounded that objects and occurrences like storms were just ordinary things without human or divine properties. We dismissed the threatening gods of volcanoes and hurricanes but with them went the comforting spirits of trees and herbs. Then followed the so-called scientific revolution. Before, during, and after this time, irrespective of labels, enquiring minds continued to investigate the world around them and this is true science. The scientific revolution was not a change in this activity but rather a change in how science viewed itself and the cosmos. It changed the perception of the universe from that of a living whole to a dead machine and perhaps this is the inherent flaw which led to lifeless products. There was a string of new inventions with the industrial revolution but with them came canned food with synthetic flavourings and cosmetics with chemical preservatives to extend the shelf-life of cheaper ingredients. There were synthetic perfumes (the first famous one was Chanel No. 5), chemical dyes, household cleaning products and medical drugs, all previously made from herbs. Scientists learned to analyse the components of herbs to select the active ingredients and synthesize them, and then businessmen convinced the public and doctors that the synthetics were preferable. Herbs had been tainted with images of witchcraft, superstition, and folklore and gradually the use and even the knowledge of herbs faded away in the great admiration for laboratory science.

Eventually the pendulum began to swing back.

Now we are returning to a more balanced middle

ground, some scientists – especially physicists – find common ground with ancient philosophies such as Taoism with regard to understanding the forces of the universe. As we again draw closer to nature our concept of a herb has expanded in line with its original meaning.

My gardening began with a strong desire to grow things but with only a vague notion of how to begin. As a child in Edmonton, Canada, I made the classically terrible dog's dinner rock gardens. I hauled home large stones where the pile was tolerated but the donated plants usually died as I had no understanding of how to nurture them.

Despite my ignorance and failure, the desire to grow things remained. In my first balcony flat in London, I grew a row of sweet peas in plastic coffee cups, intoxicated with the idea of creating a wall of the sweet-scented flowers. But I just dug the soil from a large, communal shrubbery and in the hard, caked soil they too quickly expired.

When a visitor gave me my first gardening book, *The Small Garden* by CE Phillips I was amazed to discover the depth of my ignorance. From then on I read every gardening book I could get.

Then I began to learn about herbs. They too, were useful plants, but also beautiful. In my teens, I had fluctuated between wanting to be an astronomer and an artist, settling for design as a sort of middle ground. Herbs satisfied both these interests. A scientific attitude helps the understanding of the nutritional and medical properties of herbs, while designing a herb garden, collecting and using their aromatic and colourful leaves and flowers, gladdens the heart of the artist latent in us all.

This gardening experience had wider benefits. The earthiest of subjects, it still gives me great pleasure to have my hands in healthy friable soil and to marvel at the mysteries of germination. There is the physical exercise of gardening and the benefits to health and appearance of using herbs. Emotions benefit, too, as frustrations drop away in the company of herbs and there is the soothing effect of a massage with aromatic plant essences. Mentally, the calming atmosphere of a herb garden is an excellent place to sit and solve problems.

Now the word 'herb' is more an expression of cultural attitudes and activities than a precise category. Herbs are persuasive teachers and they will open as many doors for exploration as you allow them to.

1
HERB LEAVES

The leaf is the part of a herb plant most commonly used, and from it we have culinary, cosmetic, medicinal, aromatic, decorative and household uses. There is also the odd, unexpected encounter – for example, painters like Gainsborough and Constable used parsley leaves as a model for trees in their landscape paintings. Also, a desire for aromatic herb leaves can claim to have affected history. In the sixteenth century, Cardinal Wolsey's palace at Hampton Court began to outshine Henry VII's so charges were drawn up against him which included extravagant expenses. A major complaint concerned his purchase of vast amounts of the aromatic leaves of sweet flag (*Acorus calamus*) for strewing on the floors of his many rooms.

A herb garden appeals to all the senses and leaves are the major contributor to these pleasures as they offer such a wide range of colours, textures, sizes and scents. For me the greatest of these is their fragrance. Some are sweet like bergamot, chamomile, eau-de-cologne mint, sweet myrtle and southernwood; some are savoury like tarragon, thyme and sage; some are clean and fresh like lemon verbena, spearmint, angelica and the apple-scented leaves of sweet briar after a light rain; some have a medicinal scent, like camphor leaf, and some are pungent, like wormwood and santolina.

To smell a leaf, it is usually necessary to press it hard enough to break the cell walls of the tiny glands holding the aromatic essential oils, thus releasing them to the air. Usually a gentle rubbing will suffice. In some leaves, though, like sweet myrtle, the scent pockets are deeply imbedded so a little more pressure is required to release the spicy orange fragrance. Hot sun will draw the scented essence from the leaves of several herbs as they evaporate to create a protective aura around the plant in certain conditions. Hence the summer aroma of marjoram and thyme on the hillsides of Greece.

There are several different leaf scents within a single species, for example, among the thymes we find the scent of common thyme, lemon thyme, the caraway scent of *Thymus herba barona,* the sweet-piny scent of *Thymus azoricus* and the fruity sweetness of *T. vulgaris* 'Fragrantissimus'.

In herbs, leaf sizes range from the tiny $1/10$ in (2 mm) leaves of *Mentha requinii* (the Corsican mint), to the 3 ft (1 m) elephant ears of Elecampane *(Inula helenium),* the herb Helen of Troy was collecting when she was abducted.

Then there is the texture of herb leaves: the sensuous, velvety leaves of the marsh mallow plant; the knobbly leaves of sage, and the rough leaves of comfrey and borage with their prickly hairs.

For a spectrum of leaf colour, herbs would be difficult to surpass. We find bright green lemon balm; the steely blue of Jackman's blue rue; the silver of curry plant; the strong yellow of golden moneywort or creeping Jenny (*Lysimachia nummularia aurea);* the vibrant purple of dark opal basil; plus a full range of variegated leaves. *Salvia tricolor* has pink, cream and green leaves while a leaf of the variegated form of purple sage can display purple, dark green, pink, peach and cream.

THE FUNCTION OF LEAVES

A leaf is a factory for photosynthesis; the most important process for life on the planet as it provides all our food (the entire food chain depends on plants), much of our energy (oil, natural gas and coal begin as organic material) and some of our oxygen (a by-product of photosynthesis). A leaf accomplishes this by trapping sunlight which excites the green molecules of chlorophyll in the leaf.

There is beautiful meaning in the word chlorophyll; *chloros* is Greek for green, and *philo* means loving or *philos* means beloved. So, we have beloved green or green love, a poetic summation of herbs and their offerings.

When the green molecules of chlorophyll are excited by sunlight, the leaf converts water, which it draws up from the soil via the roots and carbon dioxide inhaled

18

from the air through tiny holes in the leaf called stomata, into sugars (food for the plant) and oxygen which it exhales back through the stomata to our benefit.

Each stomata opens into an internal air sack which links with others creating a spongy 'lung' inside the leaf. On a dry, hot day there is more water vapour in the leaf than outside so it passes out through the stomata. This process is called transpiration. In hot weather, a birch tree standing in open ground with 200,000 leaves has been found to lose 100 gallons of moisture a day. Though the stomata can close to a fine slit, which they usually do at night, transpiration still occurs as the evaporation cools the air around the plant.

The water lost by transpiration is replaced by absorption through the roots. If the loss is greater than the intake, because the ground is dry or too cold, or a plant has just been transplanted and the roots have not yet caught hold, or it has no roots because it is a cutting, then the plant withers and may die. Some assistance is offered by mist spraying the leaves. Herbs do not absorb moisture through their leaves, or at least very little, but the mist will stop the transpiration of the existing moisture in the leaf.

Sometimes a large-leaved herb like sweet basil will wilt in the day, even when the soil is damp, because the water transpires more rapidly than it can be taken up by the roots. Misting the leaves at the hottest, driest time of day will help, but the plant will revive at night when the air is cooler because absorption has time to catch up with transpiration.

In winter the lack of sunlight makes it unnecessary for leaves to remain on the plant and in autumn the centre of the herb will reabsorb some of the goodness in the leaf. This process diminishes their flavour and therapeutic values and also causes changes in the pigments or colours. A few thymes take on a bronze tint after a cold spell but sages tend to turn mottled and unattractive. It is mainly the leaves of trees and shrubs that give such a farewell blaze of colours. Following the leaf changes, the plant grows a layer of tissue over the base of each leafstalk cutting off the water supply. When the leaf is dry a gust of wind will finally separate it from the plant.

With a variegated plant such as gold variegated sage, the pale yellow or white areas are not photosynthesizing as this only happens in the green areas, so these plants are weaker. This is why they usually need more sunlight and also why, if a stronger green shoot appears, it should be removed – otherwise it will dominate the variegated part and eventually replace it.

Several herbs have evergreen leaves which give plant colour and form to the herb garden in winter. These include: bay (green and gold), box (dwarf and variegated), chamomile (perennial forms), curry plant (*Helichrysum angustifolium*), feverfew (green and gold), hyssop, lavender, rosemary, rue, sage, santolinas, southernwood, sweet myrtle (*Myrtus communis* 'Tarentina'; said to be hardy though I find it only hardy in sheltered spots), thyme, wall germander (*Teucrium chamaedrys*), wild strawberry and winter savory. These plants should be called 'winter-green' rather than 'evergreen' as they replace their leaves in the spring. But with some of these plants, like hyssop and a few lavenders, (sometimes called semi-evergreen), their leaves barely hang on over the winter. Towards the end of the leafcycle, in late winter, they look a little dismal so you would not want to feature them in your winter planning.

Several other herbs appear green throughout the winter in mild seasons because they produce new shoots in the autumn which over-winter. Varieties of marjoram and oregano, angelica, fennel, salad burnet, sorrel, welsh onion and everlasting onion offer these occasional young autumn leaves which can all give an unexpected fillip to winter salads.

DESIGNING WITH HERB LEAVES

Hedges

Some of the evergreen herbs can be used to create a hedge in a garden. Box is excellent, though dwarf box is very slow growing. Its roots seldom expand outward so it does not encroach on neighbouring plants. Rosemary and curry plant are very attractive but are best grown in sheltered areas as a cold winter kills parts or all of the plants. Lavender, santolina and southernwood also offer good colours plus scent. They are a little hardier than rosemary and curry plant but will still be damaged by a severe winter. Shrubby thymes and the upright wall germander are reliable plants reaching a height of around 12 in (30 cm).

Decide before planting whether you wish to let the plants grow to their natural height (this would suit rosemary, though a little clipping will encourage bushy side growth), or whether to clip them to a set height and width which suits the santolina and box. Herbs whose flowers are valued, like lavender, are allowed to flower and are then clipped. When planting, as a rough guide, plant the herbs a distance apart which is two-thirds of their eventual height. For example, plant 3 ft (1 m) lavenders 2 ft (60 cm) apart.

Knot Gardens

The various colours of evergreen herb leaves can be used to make the pattern of woven ribbons of plants found in a knot garden. Similar to the effect of a formal path design in a garden of herbs, the geometric patterns of a knot garden give a rich contrast to the exuberant informality of many herb plants; an oasis of clipped discipline among the carefree and bountiful wild plants. It can be the focal point of your herb garden or a feature on its own. Even a small knot garden, well kept, gives an air of maturity to an entire garden.

It is wise to start with a small area as it needs regular tending to keep it looking good. About 6 x 6 ft (2 x 2 m) is the smallest into which you can thread a pattern of plants, though at this size the plants need to be clipped down to 6 in cubed (15 cm^3) bands which is difficult to maintain. An 8 x 8 ft (2.5 x 2.5 m) or 9 x 9 ft (2.75 x 2.75 m) area will allow for ribbons 9–12 in cubed (22.5–30 cm^3).

For pattern inspiration, look to old herbals or the art and artifacts of cultures which featured geometric styles such as North and South American Indians, Arabic and Chinese decorations or Hindu mandalas. It is important to achieve a balance between a simple and an intricate plan. A pattern of separate geometric beds is called a *parterre* and even though they can be very elaborate, as in some French gardens, to me they don't have the extra dimension of the movement that is created by interlocking

22

flowing ribbons of plants, weaving over and under each other to create the pattern. I have found that three colours of plants within an outer border of box give the richest pattern which remains distinct. Box is a perfect plant because it responds so beautifully to clipping and grows slowly. To achieve a colour range, santolina is a good choice because it, too, clips well and offers a silver leaved form (*S. incana* or *S. chamaecyparissus*), a green form (*S. virens*) and a willow coloured form (*S.* 'Lemon Queen'). Using three varieties of one species should give uniform growth and leaf size.

Plan your pattern carefully on grid paper making sure you mark the thickness of the ribbons of herbs and show which ribbon crosses 'over' and which crosses 'under'. Keep this drawing for future reference when you come to clip the herbs. Choose a site in full sunlight with excellent drainage and, if necessary, incorporate extra grit to a depth of 18 in (45 cm). Be meticulous about clearing the weeds from the area. Mark your design out carefully with chalk or sand and use a card template for small repeated shapes. Set plants 6–9 in (15–22.5 cm) apart. When they are large enough to clip, you can shape each plant into a square or curved section. Make the first cutting in late spring to encourage bushy growth and emphasize the movement of one ribbon 'crossing' over another by clipping a gentle humpback shape to the 'top' ribbon. If the 'lower' ribbon of herbs is clipped to slope downward before it stops either side of the 'upper' ribbon, it encourages the illusion of passing underneath. Make the last clipping in late summer so that the new growth will have time to harden before the first frosts.

PROPAGATION

Many herbs can be propagated from leaf and stem cuttings by taking a shoot of the plant and rooting it to form a new plant. This method guarantees the same characteristics of the parent plant, such as leaf and flower colour, flavour and habit of growth, and is necessary for named varieties of species. Plants from seed are more variable. For example, common sage can be grown from seed but the purple or gold leaf form needs to be grown from cuttings. Cuttings are classified in three groups: softwood, semi-hardwood and hardwood.

Softwood cuttings are taken from the current season's growth which has not yet hardened. The ideal time is either late spring, from new growth, or late summer, after flowering. Use sturdy, healthy pieces 2–4 in (5–10 cm) long with several leaves and without flowers or flower buds. If you are propagating a coloured leaf form, select a shoot with good colouring. For most plants cut just below a leaf node (the junction of leaf to stem) because there is a group of special cells which promote growth located there. Make a clean cut without ragged edges. Remove the leaves from the lower third taking care not to peel the stems which might allow entry to infections.

Softwood cuttings wilt quickly and must be planted soon after cutting. Open ground, in a sheltered spot out of constant sunlight, is always suitable for planting cuttings. Work in extra peat and sand to create the loose open soil which favours root formation. The base of the cutting can be dipped in hormone rooting powder to encourage root formation but for most herbs it is not necessary. If you do use a rooting compound, shake off the excess powder as too much can be more detrimental than using none. The leaves must be sprayed or misted twice a day for the first few days and thereafter on dry days because they will transpire moisture from their leaves but will not have roots to draw up replenishing supplies. They normally take about six weeks to root with soil temperature as the main determining factor. Sage and pelargoniums (scented leaf geraniums) take four weeks.

Alternatively, cuttings can be grown in containers, which gives greater control over their environment and flexibility in their positioning. Aim for a minimum soil temperature of 55–64°F (13–18°C); 'warmer is quicker'. When the cuttings have begun to grow, pot into individual pots with nutrients supplied, or plant outdoors giving them a sheltered position with some sun, though avoid strong mid-day sun at first. As with all plant dealings try to avoid shocks for the herb like sudden changes of temperature, light levels, etc. Make any change a gradual procedure.

Semi-hardwood cuttings are taken from new growth which has begun to firm up at the base. These are usually taken mid-summer to mid-autumn from shrubby herbs such as rosemary and sweet myrtle. Follow instructions as for softwood cuttings.

Hardwood cuttings are taken from the woody parts of shrubs and trees in mid to late autumn and given the winter to slowly develop roots, usually outside in the open ground. Follow details as for softwood cuttings.

Herbs to Grow from Cuttings

Bay (needs bottom heat; *i.e.* warmed soil), box (can take a year or longer to root), curry plant, hyssop varieties, lavender varieties, lemon verbena (in May), marjorams, myrtle, pelargoniums, rosemary varieties, rue varieties, sage varieties, santolinas, tarragon (French), thyme varieties (take small cuttings, 1–1½ in [2.5–4 cm]), winter savory and prostrate winter savory (take small cuttings, 1–1½ in [2.5–4 cm]) and wormwood varieties. Choose soft, semi-hard or hardwood cuttings depending on the time of year you are working and the available material.

HARVESTING LEAVES

A few fresh leaves can be picked whenever required in the growing season and a serving of evergreen leaves can be picked any time of the year. But for leaves destined for storage it is important to pick them at the time of optimum flavour and therapeutic qualities. This is affected by the time of day and season of the year. The best time for most leaves is morning when the dew has evaporated but before the sun has fully ascended. Damp leaves may go mouldy but the hot sun draws out the valuable plant essences. The best season is just before the plant flowers because after this some of the goodness from the leaves goes into flower and seed production.

Make certain you are confident of the variety you are picking, especially if collecting plants from the wild. This is essential both for safety (you won't wish to poison anyone) and for conservation (don't mistakenly pick an endangered species).

Pick only healthy leaves without blemish, yellowing or insect damage. When picking leaves from a perennial herb, try to leave at least two thirds of the leaves on the plant so it can continue to grow. Chives can be cut down to 2 in (5 cm) which will allow regrowth. With tall plants like marsh mallow, pick the upper portions. For small-leaved plants like marjoram and thyme cut whole stems to dry and then separate the individual leaves later.

PRESERVING

As soon as a leaf is separated from its mother plant, individual cells start to die as their supply of moisture and nutrients is cut off. Enzymes which previously helped to create active constituents now begin to break down these substances so flavour and medicinal virtues deteriorate on a sliding scale. One of the beauties of growing your own herbs is that you can have the freshest and most flavoursome herbs by picking them at the last minute. If this is not possible, herbs can be kept in good condition for a few days by placing them in the refrigerator, with air in a tightly closed plastic bag. This works well with a bunch of parsley. Putting herbs in a jar of water out of sunlight will help for a few hours but it is keeping a moist atmosphere around the leaves which maintains them longest.

For leaves to be stored, the sooner the drying or freezing begins, the more flavour and green colour can be preserved. The speed of the dry process is limited, however, because the moisture must be removed gradually from a leaf. Drying in an oven evaporates the water too quickly and the essential oils, responsible for flavour and fragrance, are lost.

Freezing retains colour and flavour well and is a fast

and convenient method for culinary herbs although some medical herbalists say it is not suitable for therapeutic herbs. It is very useful for the delicate-leaved herbs which do not dry well, like basil, chervil, chives, fennel, parsley, salad burnet, sweet cicely and tarragon. If they are from your own garden and have not been sprayed nor grown near car fumes, or made unsuitable by animals or children, you can probably judge that it is not necessary to wash them. Just pack them in plastic bags singly or in mixtures, such as a bouquet garni, and label.

Some people recommend blanching (dipping the leaf in boiling water to reduce the surface bacteria), which may be necessary for long-term storage and for large leaves like sorrel. But it is also said that ten minutes of boiling is necessary to kill all bacteria so it seems to me that its value would be minimal and it would not improve the flavour of the herb. If you wish to do it, rinse in cold water after dipping and pat or shake dry.

Herbs such as chives and parsley can be chopped and put in an ice-cube, topped up with water. When the cubes are frozen, remove them from the ice-cube tray and pack them in bags to store in the freezer. A normal ice-cube holds 1 tbsp (15 ml) of chopped herb and 1 tbsp (15 ml) of water. The frozen cube can be added to soups, stews or other liquid dishes or, if the water is unsuitable, place the cube in a sieve overnight to melt the ice and drain the herb.

The traditional method for preserving leaves, however, is to dry them. Many dry well, including mint, bay, rosemary, sage, thyme, savory and hyssop. Lay the leaves on muslin stretched over a box to allow air to circulate. Place them in a dust-free, warm, ventilated room out of direct sunlight as this will cause essential oils to evaporate. Hang stems of leaves such as rosemary, marjoram, savory and thyme in small bunches (say ten stems), stem upwards, and place an open paper bag over them if the area is dusty.

Bay is unusual in that it is one herb leaf which is better dry than fresh because the changes which take place when the leaf is detached from the plant improve its flavour rather than diminish it. It reaches optimum flavour four or five days after being picked after which it is somewhat reduced.

The ideal drying environment is a temperature of 90°F (32°C) for the first 24 hours and 75–80°F (24–26°C) thereafter. Leaves will take about four days at these temperatures. Allow one to two weeks at cooler temperatures for thick leaves.

When completed, the leaves will be paper dry but hopefully still green. Remove them from their stems and keep whole until required as this will retain flavour longer. Store in dark, airtight, glass bottles away from sunlight, moisture, dust and excessive heat. Metal and plastic containers are not advisable as they may affect the chemistry of a herb. Certain leaves such as marsh mallow and lady's mantle are hygroscopic when dried which means they absorb moisture from the air. This can reactivate their enzymes enough to cause chemical deterioration so avoid storing these for too long. The moisture-absorbing property of these herbs is, however, put to good use when used in soothing skin creams.

Most dried herbs deteriorate after a year, but by then

the next year's crop is available. Put old sweet herbs in with pot pourri and sprinkle pungent herbs on seed trays to discourage mice. Failing that, add them to the compost heap.

The flavour of herbs can also be preserved in substances which absorb flavours such as oils, fats and alcohols (including vinegar which is made from alcohol). For culinary purposes vegetable oils and vinegars can be flavoured with herbs to add an extra dimension to recipes.

Infusing an Oil with Herbs

Use one part herb to eight parts oil (by volume). Use unheated vegetable oil without a strong flavour such as sunflower or safflower although the matter is open to experimentation: olive is interesting infused with basil for special recipes like pesto and a dressing for sliced tomatoes.

Pound clean, fresh herbs in a mortar. Add a little oil and mix well. Pour into a clean glass jar with the remaining oil, cover and store for two weeks, stirring or shaking daily. Strain and bottle. Decorate with a sprig of the herb used.

If you are feeling creative, experiment with a blend of two or three herbs, steeped in succession. Savoury herbal oils can be used in salad dressings, marinades, for browning meats, softening vegetables and stir-frying, but begin with small amounts until their individual strengths become familiar.

Sweet almond and grape seed oil can be used to infuse sweet scented leaves for use in cosmetic recipes.

Savoury herb leaves best used for oils are basil, fennel,

marjorarn, mint, rosemary, tarragon, thyme, savory and the garlic bulb. Purple basil and bronze fennel give subtle burgundy/purple shades to the oil. Good sweet herb leaves for oils are young bergamot leaves, eau-de-cologne mint, lemon verbena, and sweet myrtle leaves (bruise the leaves first).

Infused Vinegars

Loosely fill a glass jar with bruised fresh leaves of the selected herb. Use cider vinegar or wine vinegar and have it warm but not hot. Pour into a jar of leaves right to the top and cap with an acid-proof lid (cleaned pickle or mayonnaise jars and lids are suitable). Place on a sunny window ledge, or if that is not available, a warm place and shake daily for two weeks. Test for flavour; if a stronger taste is required strain and save the vinegar and repeat with fresh herb leaves. When satisfied, save as it is or strain through two layers of muslin and rebottle. You can add a fresh sprig of the herb for identification and visual appeal but expect this to make the flavour a little stronger. Use in salad dressings, marinades, gravies and sauces. Even more than herbal oils, these herbal vinegars can be more potent than anticipated (especially home-made tarragon vinegar), so begin by adding a few drops to your normal vinegar until you familiarize yourself with their effects.

Basil, bay, chervil, dill, fennel, lemon balm, marjoram, mint, rosemary, savory, tarragon and thyme can all be used. Purple basil and bronze fennel give stunning rich shades of ruby and burgundy to the vinegars.

31

Herb Butters and Cheese

The composition of fats make these products excellent vehicles for absorbing the flavours of herbs. The method called *enfleurage* involves layers of fats combined with layers of flowers to absorb their delicate perfumes. Butter and soft cheeses can be treated in the same way.

Choose strongly-flavoured herbs such as chervil, chives, garlic, parsley, rosemary, sage, salad burnet, tarragon and thyme.

Use about 2 tbsp (30 ml) finely chopped fresh herbs to ½ lb (225 g) of butter or vegetable spread. Soften the butter and beat the herbs in until smooth. Set aside for two hours to allow the herb flavour to permeate the butter. Shape into moulds if desired and chill before serving.

HERBS FOR HEALTH AND BEAUTY

When the primary aspects of lifestyle are in order, the individual qualities of many herbs can be used to enhance the appearance of our skin and hair. Herbs have a part to play in creating a healthy diet, by offering sugar and salt substitutes, caffeine-free drinks, and even massage oils for exercized muscles.

Herbal Nutrition for Skin Care

Raw materials required by the body to neutralize elements which cause ageing and loss of elasticity in the skin include Vitamins A, betacarotene, C and E, some amino acids and selenium.

A rich source of Vitamin A can be found in fresh dandelion leaves, most beneficial taken raw in salads and sandwiches. Vitamin A is also present in watercress, American landcress and parsley. (A little parsley each day is highly beneficial but avoid an excess as it contains apiol, an alkaloid harmful in large quantities.) Vegetables with Vitamin A include Swiss chard and seakale beet, broccoli, carrots, spinach, turnip tops, tomatoes and radishes, while kale is almost as rich in the vitamin as cod liver oil. Fruits with orange-coloured skins, including apricots, oranges and peaches, contain a little Vitamin A.

Vitamin E should be taken with Vitamin A as the body needs one to make use of the other. Vitamin E is present in leafy, green herbs and vegetables, in wheatgerm, green peas and beans. It is most useful taken with Vitamin B2 and they are found together in wheatgerm, kale, Swiss chard, cress and legumes.

Herbs containing Vitamin C include the leaves of dandelion, watercress, lady's smock and nasturtium, and the fruits of strawberries, blackcurrants, grapes and apples of which Bramley's seedling has the highest Vitamin C content. Of the vegetables, tomatoes, curly kale and broccoli are rich in Vitamin C.

Skin Care – Using Herbal Extracts

Skin is constantly under attack from external agents such as the sun's ultraviolet radiation, environmental radiation, drying winds, cigarette smoke, air pollutants, including ozone and sulphur dioxide, pesticides, heavy metals, petrol fumes, some cosmetic ingredients and several household chemicals.

The first line of defence is to avoid as many of these pollutants as possible. The second is to clean, protect and nourish the skin with pure herbal products. To extract the useful properties of herbs four methods have been developed.

1. **Pulverize.** Use a pestle and mortar (or blender) to mash, grind or bruise the plant parts, breaking the fibres to make the essential oils or other therapeutic parts more accessible.

2. **Infusion.** Put 1½ handfuls of fresh herbs or 1 oz (25 g) dried herbs in a china, glass or enamel pot (avoid aluminium or copper). Boil 1 pt (600 ml) of pure water (rainwater, mineral water or distilled water), pour over the herb immediately, then cover with a lid to stop the therapeutic vapours escaping. Steep for at least 30 minutes, then filter through a fine plastic strainer or coffee filter. It will keep for up to three days in the the refrigerator.

3. **Decoction.** This system is generally used for the tougher parts of herbs such as roots, stems and seeds. 1 oz (25 gm) of the herb, chopped if necessary, is put into a pyrex or enamel saucepan and boiled with 1 pt (600 ml) of pure water. Bring to the boil then simmer gently for 30 minutes by which time the liquid should be reduced by half. If more has evaporated, top up with water to make ½ pt (300 ml). Cool, strain and bottle. Store in the refrigerator and use within three days.

4. **Maceration.** This method is used for herbs which would lose some of their valuable properties if heated. It involves steeping the herbs in oil, vinegar, wine or alcohol, often in the presence of sunlight to speed the process. Some of the herbal properties will be released within a few hours but most require two or three weeks with daily

stirring or shaking of the oil, vinegar or alcohol to have the maximum absorption. Some herbalists leave the plant parts macerating until the liquid is needed.

Macerations required for aromatic purposes can be judged by scent or taste. If the aroma is insufficient after two weeks, the first plant parts are removed and fresh plants are added, repeating the process. As the liquids used have preserving qualities, macerations will keep several months.

Herbal Baths

The easiest way to use herbs to benefit our skin and well-being is to add a handful to the bath or sprinkle in a few drops of the herb's essential oil. Herbs can be chosen for deep cleansing action, to stimulate the circulation, or to relax the body for a peaceful night's sleep. They can be added to improve specific skin conditions, or just for the pleasure of their fragrance.

Dismiss the desire to fling the leaves into the water with romantic ideas of Ophelia. They cling to you and clog the drain. Instead put a generous handful of fresh or dried herbs in the centre of a handkerchief and tie up the corners to make a bag. Amounts are not critical. Use a single herb or a mixture of those which have the therapeutic properties you prefer. By adding fine ground oatmeal or bran to the bag you can make a body scrub and use it to rub your body near the end of the bathing time.

Another quick method is to use three or four tea bags of herbs available as tea bags such as chamomile or peppermint.

A little more work will give you greater benefits,

however. More therapeutic properties will be extracted from the herbs if they are first boiled in a covered saucepan for 15 minutes and the strained liquid is added to your bath water. This decoction can be stored for up to three days in a refrigerator.

Try to keep the bath temperature around body heat because if the bath is too hot the skin will be perspiring and possibly not absorbing the beneficial properties of the herbs, although you will at least be taking them through inhalation. It is known that essential oils (released from the herbs by steam) can pass the skin barrier but there is presently insufficient research to show under what conditions this does or does not happen.

Suitable herbs for the bath are as follows:

Deep cleansing herbs: borage, lemon balm, meadowsweet and sage; also rose petals.

Deodorant herbs: cleavers or goosegrass (*Galium aparine*), lovage, parsley and sage.

Relaxing bath herbs: catnip, hops, meadowsweet, valerian; also flowers of chamomile, cowslips, jasmine, lime blossom, mullein and violets.

Stimulating bath herbs: basil, bay, fennel, lemon verbena, lemon thyme, marjoram, mint, stinging nettles (boiling will remove their sting), pennyroyal, peppermint, pine, rosemary, sage and thyme.

Facial Steams

A facial steam is an inexpensive way to provide deep cleansing. The perspiration from the heat improves circulation and helps eliminate toxins and other waste products. The essential oils released by the herbs will benefit the exterior of the skin and be absorbed when inhaling. When the skin is not perspiring, the open pores or hair folicles may absorb the essential oils internally via the skin and lymph system.

Fennel, nettle, rosemary and lime blossom improve circulation and encourage deep cleansing.

Borage, houseleek, lady's mantle, marsh mallow (roots and leaves), parsley, salad burnet, sorrel, violet leaves and flowers, plus cornflowers, are soothing and softening for dry sensitive skin.

Geranium (herb robert), horsetail, sage, yarrow, crushed lupin seeds and calendula petals help refine pores and remove dead skin cells which is especially beneficial to oily skins.

Lemon verbena, dandelion, red clover (leaves and flowers), tansy (leaves and flowers) and elderflowers are used to revive mature or sallow skins.

When giving yourself a facial steam, first tie back your hair, remove your makeup and clean your skin as normal. Put 2 handfuls of fresh leaves (or 3 tbsp [45 ml] dried) in a basin and pour on 3 pts (1.8 l) boiling water. Stir briefly with a wooden spoon. Then hold your face about a foot (30 cm) above the basin (18 in [45 cm] if you have sensitive skin) and make a tent with a towel over your head to confine the steam. Close your eyes and maintain this for 10–15 minutes.

Rinse with tepid water and then cold water a few minutes later to gradually close the pores. Dab on an infusion of peppermint, sage or yarrow leaves or elderflower to tighten the pores. Avoid dramatic changes of temperature for an hour or two.

Do not use a facial steam if you have thread veins, serious skin disorders, asthma or other breathing difficulties, or heart problems.

Making a Herbal Face Pack

Double deep cleaning can be achieved if a face pack is applied after a facial steam and before the pores have closed. It works deeply to draw impurities to the surface and stimulates circulation.

Select any of the above herbs suitable for your skin to make a mask. Soak 2 handfuls of fresh or 3 tbsp (1.5 ml) dried herbs (soften by soaking in boiled water for several hours) with 2 tbsp (30 ml) pure water and liquidize for a few seconds. Apply this wet mixture as is or add Fuller's earth or ground almonds until a suitable paste is created. Apply it to damp skin and rest with your feet higher than your legs to encourage greater blood supply to the face. Place cooling eye pads of cucumber or cold chamomile tea bags against your closed eyelids. Leave mask for 20–30 minutes before rinsing off with warm water. Finish with a toner of witch hazel or a pore closing infusion such as elderflower water, peppermint, sage or yarrow.

Marsh Mallow Hand Cream
2 oz (50 g) marsh mallow (leaves or root slices)
2 oz (50 g) lady's mantle
2 pts (1.2 l) water
1½ fl oz (40 ml) almond oil
1 oz (25 g) beeswax
1½ tbsp (22.5 ml) clear honey

1 tsp (5 ml) wheatgerm oil
1 tbsp (15 ml) avocado or hazelnut oil to increase
penetration (use more wheatgerm or almond if this is
not available)
8 drops of geranium, lavender or sandalwood essential
oil (optional)

Simmer the herbs in the water for ½ hour in a covered
saucepan. Set aside to cool keeping the lid on. Melt the
almond oil, avocado or hazelnut oil and beeswax over
gentle heat. Remove from heat. Stir in the honey until
smooth. Strain the herbal decoction through double
muslin or a coffee filter paper and add this to the wheatgerm oil, beating constantly. Stir in the essential oil and
pour into a wide mouth jar. Cool, cover, label and date.

Chapped Skin Soother
4 large aloe vera leaves (or 2 tbsp aloe vera gel; or
houseleek)
4 leaves lady's mantle
4 leaves comfrey
1 tbsp (15 ml) honey
1 tsp (5 ml) infused comfrey oil (see p. 30) or almond oil
oatmeal

Peel the aloe vera leaves and pound together with the
lady's mantle and comfrey (which contains allentoin, a
protein which encourages cell renewal). With a gentle
heat, melt the honey in the infused comfrey (or almond)
oil and then beat into the herbs. Add enough of the finely
ground oatmeal to make a paste.

Apply thickly to the hands, keep on overnight wearing cotton gloves. Store excess for a week to 10 days in a refrigerator.

Ivy Cellulite Cream
1 oz (25 g) ivy
1 cup water
2 tsp (10 ml) beeswax
1 tsp (5 ml) emulsifying wax
1 tbsp (15 ml) hazelnut oil
1 tsp (5 ml) avocado oil
8 drops each of essential oils of fennel, geranium and
rosemary (each has a role to play in improving
circulation and aiding the removal of cellulite)

Boil the ivy in the water until it is reduced to 4 tbsp (60 ml). Melt the waxes together and stir in the warmed oils, blending thoroughly. Beat in the ivy decoction until smooth, cool a little, stir in the essential oils and pour into a wide mouth jar. Cover, label and date.

Massage this daily into areas of cellulite with a vigorous stroke toward the heart and a lighter stroke outward.

Hair Care
Herb leaves used to condition dry hair include comfrey, marsh mallow, stinging nettles, parsley and sage; plus burdock root and elderflowers. Herbs for greasy hair are horsetail, lemon balm, mints, rosemary, southernwood, witchhazel and yarrow; plus calendula petals, lavender and lemon juice.

Herbs to add body and lustre include goosegrass,

horsetail, parsley, rosemary, sage, southernwood, stinging nettle and watercress; plus calendula petals, lime flowers and nasturtium.

These herbs can be used in three ways: as a pre-shampoo oil; in a shampoo and as an after-shampoo rinse.

To make a pre-shampoo lotion, start with an infused herbal oil or macerate a selected herb or herbs in a vegetable oil (see p. 30). Alternatively, add a few drops of the essential oil of the chosen herb, if available, to a small amount of vegetable oil. Then pour a little of the warmed herbal oil on to the hands and massage into the scalp drawing the oil out along the hair strands. Cover the head with foil and a shower cap and wrap in a hot towel (wrung out in hot water), replacing the towel as it cools. Maintain this for 20–30 minutes for greatest penetration, then wash off with a mild shampoo.

For shampoo, add a few drops of the essential oil of a selected herb to a bottle of mild, fragrance-free shampoo. For a single shampooing, mix one application of shampoo with a tbsp of a strong decoction in a cup and apply as normal.

Finally, an after-shampoo rinse is made from a strong decoction, cooled to blood heat. The herbs listed above for body and lustre are especially useful for giving extra shine.

To Darken Hair

A strong decoction of sage leaves, sage with rosemary leaves, or sage and dried raspberry leaves can be used as a gentle dark hair rinse.

Teeth

Rub a sage leaf over your teeth and gums to clean and polish them.

AROMATIC DELIGHTS

The fresh fragrance of herbs may seem like a luxury, something beyond the strictly utilitarian, but the fundamental importance of scent is only beginning to be properly recognized. The power of sweet perfumes to transform our moods is now well documented and to use the natural fresh aromas of herbs is one of the most wholesome ways to lift our spirits.

For those with a garden, the simplest way to have herbal scent around the house is to arrange vases of fresh herbs. These perfume the room and as the plant essences evaporate, they cool and purify the air. The number of ways dried herbs can be used is limited only by your imagination. In the kitchen, dried aromatic herbs can be added to oven mitts or a tea-cosy by tucking them inside the hem or a specially made pocket. Both the handling they receive and the heat they contact will release their fragrance. Use fresh-smelling herbs like mint, lemon thyme, angelica and lemon verbena.

Stick fragrant herbs in saddle bags to fling over the backs of chairs. Each time someone sits they will disturb and release the fragrance. Make two equal-sized herb pillows and join with two wide ribbons. You could fill one pillow with 'summer' scents and the other with 'winter' scents and swap when the seasons change. Place santolina, southernwood, wormwood or lavender among old books to discourage worms. Spices and the essential oils of cloves and cinnamon also work well. In fact, the ancient Egyptians protected their papyrus with cinnamon.

Sweet Myrtle Furniture Wax
2 oz (50 g) beeswax
½ pt (300 ml) turpentine
6 fl oz (175 ml) strong infusion of sweet myrtle
¼ oz (7 g) olive oil based soap

Grate beeswax into turpentine and leave to dissolve. This may take a few days. Alternatively, warm beeswax with turpentine carefully over *flameless* heat until wax melts (turpentine can easily burst into flame). Bring the sweet myrtle infusion to boiling point and stir in the grated soap until melted. Allow both mixtures to cool then blend slowly stirring until it resembles thick cream. Stir in a few drops of essential oil if desired. Pour into wide topped container and label.

Aromatic Crafts
Use twigs of aromatic herbs like rosemary, thyme and blades of sweet vernal grass or vanilla grass (*Anthoxanthum odoratum*) to make craft items like woven place mats and baskets.

Pine-scented twigs of the tamarack tree, a variety of larch, are used by the Cree Indian hunters of James Bay, northern Ontario, to make their famous duck decoys. The core of the body is composed of a ball of twigs and then the outer part is shaped like a Canada Goose. As the bird slowly dries the scent fades, but if it is submerged in hot water for 10 to 15 minutes, the fragrance returns. This can be repeated as often as necessary.

Leave any surplus prunings of aromatic herbs in a container near the hearth to throw on the fire to scent and purify the air.

Aromatic Storage

In the bedroom, stick small muslin bags of fragrant leaves in drawers and inside padded coat hangers. Choose the refreshing mint and citrus herbs and perhaps one of the more unusual artemisias like *A. camphorita* for men's clothes. And, most pleasing of all, give yourself sweet dreams by placing fragrant herbs in a sachet under your pillow. Try sweet woodruff, melilot and lady's bedstraw which all smell of new mown hay when they are dried; or dried strawberry leaves, pine needles and oakmoss for the atmosphere of an autumn woodland.

In the linen cupboard, lay them among your sheets and towels, just for the pleasure of rummaging on the shelves. Sprigs of lavender, rosemary, southernwood, alecost, dried lemon peel or root pieces of orris, elecampane, roseroot or sweet flag among clothes will scent the linen and protect it from moths.

Sweet Waters for Rinsing and Scenting Linen

Make a strong decoction of aromatic leaves or flowers in a covered pan, strain well and use as the final rinse for hand-washed articles or add to the final rinse cycle of your washing machine. Use leaves of rosemary, lemon verbena, sweet myrtle, bergamot, sweet marjoram, angelica, bay, alecost and eau-de-cologne mint or powdered root of roseroot or flowers of lavender, violets, pinks and roses. A ½ tsp (2.5 ml) of orris root dissolved in the decoction will fix the scent. The mixture can also be sprinkled on clothes before ironing. Alternatively, drops of an essential oil dissolved in a little pure alcohol (or vodka) can be added to the final rinse. Sweet waters can also be used to sprinkle around rooms or as a hair rinse to give it a subtle perfume.

HOUSEHOLD USES

The antibacterial and antifungal properties of many herb leaves give them preservative qualities which can be put to good use. Also, herbs used to discourage insect pests and mice in the kitchen mean that the use of toxic chemicals where food is stored, can be avoided.

There are many household uses with more being discovered or rediscovered. The following are some small, simple offerings:

Dried nettle leaves wrapped around moist cheeses, apples, pears and root vegetables will keep the skins smooth and moist for two or three months.

Figs will keep in good condition wrapped in mullein leaves.

Wrap joints in whole bruised sorrel leaves to tenderize meat.

A few bay leaves placed in flour and rice bins or stored with dried pulses will deter weevils.

Mice are repelled by the smell of mint and tansy leaves.

On long sea voyages, pennyroyal was added to kegs of water to help keep it sweet. Its pungent scent also repels ants. Rub a fresh sprig on the surface of a shelf, cupboard or counter top or across the ants' entrance point or route if you know it. Then leave the sprig in the cupboard, or wherever, and disturb it periodically to release more scent. Stronger scent or larger sprigs are needed for bigger ants. It does not kill the ants, but they do not like the smell and will go elsewhere to avoid it. Rue and tansy will also work but avoid touching rue as it gives some skins a nasty, long-lasting rash.

A pot of basil placed on the window is a traditional deterrent to flies, particularly the small-leaved, compact Greek basil. Bouquets of elder, tansy, mint, peppermint, rue, wormwood, mugwort, pennyroyal, hemp agrimony and chamomile can be strategically placed to deter flies. Try rubbing leaves on the woodwork around a window or door frame.

Black Silk Reviver

Boil ivy leaves and mash until water is dark. Strain and use the solution as a rinse for black silk.

Fumigation

To kill fleas and lice, burn leaves of common fleabane (*Pulicaria dysenterica*), greater fleabane (*Inula conyza*), mugwort and wormwood over low embers and encourage the fumes to fill the room (clear everyone, particularly children and pets, away and avoid breathing the fumes). Burn the dried leaf of *Eupatoria cannabium* to drive away wasps and flies.

Rust Stain Remover

Place wood sorrel leaves (*Oxalis acetosella*) in a juice extractor. Dab the juice on rust stain and soak for half an hour. Rinse and repeat if necessary.

For rust on white linen, place a slice of lemon between two sheets of tissue paper, place on the white linen rust spots and press with a hot iron; rinse and repeat as necessary.

Thyme Disinfectant

The general prunings of disinfectant herbs like thyme, juniper, eucalyptus, pine, sage, rosemary, lavender or the roots of angelica will provide a germ-killing solution with a fresh, pleasant scent. Boil the leaves and stems in water for half an hour. The higher the ratio of leaves to water, the stronger the disinfectant will be. Strain and use for washing kitchen surfaces, sinks and bathroom facilities. The addition of a little washing-up liquid will remove grease from surfaces. Store any excess in the fridge for up to one week.

GARDEN USES

Sprigs of elder and bog myrtle (*Myrica gale*) in hats minimize summer midges, and lavender or wormwood deter flies.

Comfrey Fertilizer

The excellent quality of a general fertilizer made from comfrey is due to the rich mineral content of the leaves and stems, particularly the Russian comfrey (*Symphytum uplandicum*) which has valuable amounts of potassium, magnesium, iron and calcium. The high quantity of potassium makes it a near perfect food for fruiting tomato and cucumber plants.

Make up a liquid feed by loosely filling a bucket or a water butt with a tap with comfrey leaves and then add water to cover the leaves. The comfrey then ferments in two weeks in hot weather (up to four weeks in cool weather) to produce a very smelly, brown liquid. Extract it from the tap or squeeze and pour it from the bucket and use this as a concentrated feed. Dilute it at the rate of roughly 1/3 cup to 1 gallon (4.5 l) of water.

Nettle is another herb rich in minerals, trace elements, nitrogen and iron. Process leaves in the same way as comfrey.

Elder Leaf Insecticide

Simmer 1/2 lb (225 g) leaves in 2 pts (1.2 l) of water for 1/2 hour. Stir well and then strain. Separately dissolve 1 tsp (5 ml) soap flakes or washing-up liquid in 1 pint (600 ml) of warm water. Mix with the elder water to help the solution to stick to the leaves when it is sprayed on. Use a sprayer with relatively large holes as the mixture will clog fine holes. Elder also has fungicidal properties and there are reports of its success against mildew and blackspot on roses. Rhubarb leaves roughly chopped can be prepared as an insecticide following the elder recipe. Take care with hygiene when making homemade insecticides and ensure they are properly labelled and kept safely away from children and pets.

Wormwood prepared as above has powerful insecticide

properties against larger pests such as caterpillars, flea beetles and moths, as well as aphids. But this should be diluted to half strength and only used on mature plants because of its toxic properties. An easy way to use the pungent scent of wormwood to deter insects is to lay branches of the herb along rows of carrots and onions in the vegetable garden. The leaves lie there and dry out but release their strong scent whenever they are disturbed. This can mask the carrot scent and confuse the carrot fly.

DECORATIVE USES

Botanical wreaths have been used throughout western civilization to celebrate events, honour heros, athletes and academics and to provide a focus for reflection in mourning. Herbs add an extra dimension by introducing fragrance to the wreath and with their range of leaf colour, shape and texture plus their historical connections, they can be used to create something very special.

Making a Wreath

In addition to your herbs, there are two main materials to acquire. The first is a circular base which may be of bound or plaited straw, plain or moss-covered wire, plaited raffia, twisted vine or bound aromatic twigs. These can be home made or bought from a florist. The second is a range of pins, reel (continuous) wire and stub wires (wires cut to set lengths) for attaching the herbs to the base. These are available from florists and craft shops who should be able to advise you on suitable sizes of stub wires for the stem thickness of the plants you have selected. Once a stub wire is attached to a herb stem it can be bound with gutta-percha tape, a rubber-based tape available in the natural colours of dark green, brown or white.

Fresh or dried herbs can be used but fresh herbs are more flexible and will dry satisfactorily on the wreath.

Often the base is covered with a background material such as sphagnum moss, securely bound in place with fine florist or reel wire. If a circle of one type of leaf is being applied all around the wreath, first make up bunches with a few sprigs cut to the same length. Lay them on the base and bind them with reel wire. Lay the second bunch to overlap the stems of the first facing the same direction and continue binding with the same reel wire. Proceed around the entire circle tucking the stems of the last bunch under the leaves of the first.

To add individual herbs, bend one third of a stub wire around the stem a few times and use the remaining two thirds to extend the stem and pin the herb into the base. For small sprigs like thyme, wire a few stems together with the top one-third of a fine stub wire to create a small bunch and use the remainder as a pin to hold the bunch in the base.

When displaying your herbal wreath, try to avoid direct sunlight, moisture and wind, which all shorten its attractive life. Also consider that dried hangings are not fireproof and should be displayed where there is no danger from stray sparks.

If the hanging is part of a permanent display, clean it periodically with a cool blow-dryer or a vacuum cleaner which can be put on reverse so it blows air out. Hold the open end at least 12 in (30 cm) away from the wreath.

To store a wreath, cover it loosely with tissue paper and pack carefully in a box or an opaque plastic bag to hang in a dark, dry location. A few sprigs of santolina, lavender, tansy, wormwood or pennyroyal will help keep bugs away.

Making a Garland

A garland is made in a similar fashion to a wreath using a length of string as the centre piece, or rope if the hanging is to be bulky. Measure out the length of the curve where you wish to hang the garland and cut the string to this length, allowing a little extra for a loop at each end to attach it with. Assemble your material and if you are using fresh herbs and flowers, as many garland makers do, mist spray them with water occasionally while working to keep them fresh. This way the herbs should last three days.

Select your material with an eye to colour, fragrance and scale, favouring those which last longer, like the thick leaves of box and sweet myrtle. You might perhaps decide to choose small herb leaves and flowers in soft colours. A good background would be made up of variegated box with the cream flowers of *Santolina* 'Lemon Queen', the blue-grey leaves of eucalyptus, the deep-purple flowers of lavender Hidcote, clusters of the tiny, lime-green flowers of lady's mantle (*Alchemilla mollis*, 'the flower arranger's friend'), the ½-in (1.25-cm) long, steel-blue flowers of the thistle *Eryngium tripartitum,* a small cream miniature florabunda rose called 'Cream Serena' (presently available as a cut flower from Italy) and two yarrow flowers, the cream 'Moonshine' and the relatively new 'Salmon Beauty' with apricot flowers.

Tie on the herbs with a continuous length of fuse wire. Larger leaves are put on indivdually while smaller stems, like thyme sprigs, can be bunched together in groups of three or five. Tie on the first group with the flowers facing towards the end and proceed around the base covering the first stems with the second batch, and so on. Vary the colour, leaf size and shape as you progress but maintain an overall harmony. A common error of beginners is to bunch up too many stems at the start of the garland, so try to spread it evenly. Keep turning the garland so that you work in a spiral around the central string to avoid having a front and back.

MEDICINAL USES

Herbs are humanity's most ancient healing aid with a history of several thousand years of continuous use. Even in orthodox medicine today, plants are an important source of therapeutic material. But with the tendency of medical scientists to isolate the active ingredients of herbs in order to create a more powerful medicine the side effects have also become stronger and more serious.

Another change in western medicine has been the move to specialization which means a focusing of the medic's attention on a particular area of the human body. Such work is against one of the original and fundamental ideas of healing, that of rebalancing the basic influences on our body to remove the cause of the illness. Whether these basics are labelled the four humours, the five elements or lifestyle (diet, exercise and stress levels), the principle is the same. For this reason many people are turning to complementary medicines and herbs make a contribution to several of these systems.

To treat illness with herbs, accurate diagnosis is important and to use herbal treatments it is necessary to consult a qualified medical herbalist. Even if you go to an orthodox doctor just for the diagnosis, it is important to see a qualified herbalist for a herbal prescription because individual dosage and blends of herbs vary with the circumstances of each case. Also, the secondary effects of a desirable herb may not be suitable in certain cases and no book written for the lay person can include all these eventualities. When writers describe the attributes of a herb, if there is any record of the plant being harmful to a certain condition, *e.g.* pregnancy, they must in conscience advise against its use in such circumstances even though thousands may have used it safely. A qualified herbalist, however, is more likely to know if that particular herb would be safe for you by analysing your specific circumstances.

Despite these comments, there are several herbs which can be safely used for common ailments like colds, sprains, minor burns and sore throats.

Aloe Vera

The leaf of the *Aloe vera* plant (also named *A. barbadensis*) has remarkable healing properties but it is important to have the true *A. vera* (the botanic meaning of vera is 'true, exact') because there are around 350 species and they do not share the same properties. It is a tender, succulent evergreen needing a minimum temperature of 41°F (5°C).

It makes a good houseplant as it enjoys the dry air of interiors and it is in the kitchen that it has earned its name as 'the first-aid plant'. It prefers a gritty, well-drained soil and will take sun or light shade. It can be propagated from offshoots, young plantlets which grow around the base in spring. Separate these, dry for two days and then repot them in compost made of two parts compost to one part sharp sand. Water once a week in summer, once a month in winter and repot annually in spring.

Research has isolated some active substances from the leaf but none are as effective as the fresh sap which includes all the active ingredients. The sap deteriorates rapidly when isolated so the only way to have a constant supply is to grow it at home although several health product firms are working on ways to preserve it.

Inside the leaf is a clear gelatinous sap which has an immediate soothing effect on burns and when applied, forms a clear protective seal allowing healing to take place rapidly. It has been used since at least the fourth century BC and is still commercially grown. It has attracted the interest of governments for its ability to heal radiation burns and there are reports that the US government is stockpiling *Aloe vera* in Texas for use in case of nuclear war.

For minor burns, break or cut off a leaf segment, preferably from a two-year-old plant, and touch sap directly to the burn – it instantly relieves pain and any burning sensation, forms a protective skin to stop infection and healing takes place rapidly. For larger areas, split the leaf, open it out, place the sap against the damaged skin and lightly bandage it in place. Renew this every day. Two fresh leaves crushed or sliced can be applied as a poultice for chapped and dry skin, dermatitis, eczema, sunburn, heat and radiation burns. But remember, always seek trained medical personnel for serious burns.

The soothing and healing qualities of *Aloe vera* leaf sap have long been utilized in cosmetic products. It was said to be one of Cleopatra's secret beauty ingredients and is popular today in moisturizers and hand creams, especially for dry skin, in sun-tan lotions for its cooling and healing properties and shampoos where it relieves an itchy scalp.

Comfrey

This is another leaf with remarkable healing properties. Both forms: *Symphytum officinale* and *Symphytum* x *uplandicum,* also known as *S. peregrinum,* are useful.

The leaf contains allentoin, a protein encouraging cell division, which is responsible for its healing properties. It works through the skin when applied in comfrey oint-ment, as an 'oil' or in a leaf poultice. It has had some remarkable results in speeding the healing of stubborn leg ulcers, sprains and broken bones in humans and animals, particularly horses. The ointment and oil is also healing for patches of rough skin (like those that precede eczema); aching joints, sores and skin ulcerations; tissue damaged from burns, cuts, acne and other skin conditions; sprains; and is helpful in reducing the swelling around fractures.

The only ingredient involved in making comfrey oil is the comfrey leaf. The resultant liquid which is created feels halfway between a water and an oil. To make com-frey 'oil', pick clean, dry, undamaged leaves and cut them roughly into small pieces (say 1 in [25 cm] squares). Pack as much as possible into a clean, dark jar, pressing it in around the shoulder. Apply a screw-top lid, label and date. Store for about two years and do not open it and let air in. Fermentations eventually produce an amber viscous liquid with a sediment. Decant this 'oil' into a smaller container and label. It will keep for months, probably years.

The list of beneficial vitamins and minerals in comfrey is impressive: Vitamins A, C and B12 (especially useful for vegetarians, and previously thought to be only available in meat products), calcium, potassium, phosphorus and trace minerals are all to be found. It has more protein in its leaf structure than any other known member of the vegetable kingdom, equal to soya beans and greater than cheddar cheese. Comfrey also has a reputation for remarkable healings in treating gastric ulcers and in bronchial problems, being widely used in natural tuberculosis sanatoriums of Europe and Scandinavia.

For these uses, comfrey was taken internally (as it has been for centuries) with no reported ill effects. In the 1970s, however, there was a report that large concentrated doses were carcinogenic to the liver of rats, causing worry to users. This was relieved by an announcement in the British Medical Journal (3 March 1979, page 593) evaluating the evidence of pharmacists and scientists plus the accumulated reports of herbalists. It concluded that the carcinogenic response in animals was from continuous high dosing over long periods; that liver poisoning preceded tumour development, and that the consumption in man was much lower and no instances of liver poisoning had ever been reported. It concluded that people who have in the past consumed comfrey have no cause for alarm.

Peppermint, Yarrow and Elderflowers

At the first sign of a cold take a mixture of equal parts of peppermint leaves, yarrow leaves and elderflowers (freeze or dry flowers in spring for year-round use). Infuse ½ tsp (2.5 ml) of each, dried, together in a cup of boiling water for 20 minutes. Strain and add 1 tsp (5 ml) honey. It is even more potent if you also add ¼ tsp (1.25 ml) cayenne pepper. This will decrease the intensity and the discomfort of a cold. These three herbs promote perspiration and reduce temperature which makes frequent hot drinks of the combination also a useful treatment for flu.

Sage

Purple sage is wonderful for sore throats. Make an infusion (1 oz [25 g] dried or 2 oz [50 g] fresh herb to 1 pt [570 ml] boiling water) and let it stand for at least 15 minutes. Drink ½ cup, four times a day and gargle with it anytime to relieve discomfort. Do not use sage if you are pregnant as in rare circumstances it can be abortive.

Sage aids digestion, is antiseptic and antifungal. It also contains an oestrogen-like compound which is useful for women to take in the first half of their menstrual cycle as a daily tea, especially during the menopause. It is also a nerve and blood tonic but sage should not he taken in large doses for a long period.

CULINARY USES

Herbs are the magic ingredients that can transform a routine meal into a special experience of zesty, crunchy, refreshing flavours and textures. Herbs and spices used to be necessary to preserve food and mask the often unpleasant taste and smell of meat that was less than fresh. But now we can use a much lighter hand and investigate the delicate flavours of herbs like chervil and buckler leaf sorrel, with its lemon piquancy, and experiment with combinations of flavours.

The aromatic leaves of rosemary, sage and thyme have maintained their popularity with roast meats not only because their flavours enhance those of the meats but also because they aid the digestion of meat fats.

As we grow more adventurous in preparing the cuisine of other cultures we are introduced to an even wider range of exotic flavourings. Oriental dishes are no longer just one category but the specialities of Thailand, Indonesia or Vietnam are created, each with their own distinctive use of herbs and spices.

And, finally, we are encouraged to rediscover recipes from our own national cookery; dishes where the strong flavoured leaves of lovage and smallage add body to soups and casseroles, where fennel is served in a rich sauce with salmon, and lemon balm is rubbed on game or wrapped around chicken before roasting.

Dinner Party Dishes

ROAST POUSSIN WITH HERBS *(Serves 4)*
    4 poussins (ask your butcher to bone them if you prefer)
    1 tbsp (15 ml) fresh thyme (for the stock)
    1½ pt (900 ml) good veal stock
    4 small sausages
    4 slices of bread
    1 tsp (5 ml) fresh chives
    1 tsp (5 ml) fresh marjoram
    1 tsp (5 ml) thyme
    (amounts are approximate and governed by taste, but
    keep the herbs in equal proportions)

Bone each poussin by laying, breast side down, on a chopping board. Slit the skin along the backbone from neck to tail. Working close to the bone, continue cutting down one side of the carcass cutting between the wing bone and thigh bone joints. Work around and up the other side of the rib cage until the meat has been completely removed from the bones. This sounds complicated but if you don't cut the skin, and keep it in one piece, the job is not that difficult, and well worth attempting.

Now remove the thigh bone, leaving only one bone in the leg and then sever the first two bones from the wing (use these in the stock), leaving only the upper wing bone. Leaving these bones in the bird helps to reshape the bird before cooking. Set aside until sauce is made.

Roast the bones and add them to the veal stock. Simmer for 1–2 hours. Strain and de-fat the stock. Reduce the stock to form a thick 'sauce'. Strain again, add chopped thyme leaves and season. A few drops of thyme vinegar add a special touch to the sauce.

Skin the sausages, moisten the bread with a little stock, and chop the herbs. Mix together using sufficient herbs to reach the desired aroma. The herbs may be varied: try lemon balm, winter savory, sage or tarragon.

Divide the meat between the birds and reshape them into the original whole bird form. Place on a greased tray and roast at 350°F (180°C) Mark 4 for 15 minutes or until browned and cooked through.

Serve the poussin coated with the sauce and surround with a garland of thyme flowers.

BEEF IN PASTRY   (Serves 2)

loz (25 g) butter
12–16 oz (350–450 g) beef fillet
½ lb (225 g) puff pastry
1 large chicken breast
1 tsp (5 ml) chives finely chopped
10 medium leaves good King Henry (a herb similar to spinach)
2 slices unsmoked bacon

Melt butter in pan, brown beef (approximately 2 minutes) and set aside to cool. Roll out pastry to a thickness of ¼ in (6 mm) in a square. Purée or finely mince the chicken with the chives and good King Henry leaves to form a fine paste, season lightly. Lay the bacon in the middle of the pastry and spread the chicken meat on the bacon to the size of the piece of meat being used. Place the beef on top and wrap the pastry neatly around like a parcel. It is not necessary to moisten the edges to seal the pastry if the dish is cooked immediately.

Cook in a preheated oven at 375°F (190°C) Mark 5 for 20 minutes or until the pastry browns. If the beef is required medium to well-done, the meat must be cooked longer in the browning stage or, for well-done beef, it would be necessary to roast the beef an additional 20 minutes before roasting it in the pastry. Rest for 10 minutes before carving. Serve with a whisky sauce made from cream, meat glaze and whisky reduced to required consistency.

APPLE AND LEMON BALM TERRINE (Serves 12)
7 leaves gelatine or ¾ oz (22 g) powdered gelatine
17 fl oz (475 ml) milk
1 vanilla pod
generous handful fresh lemon balm leaves
6 egg yolks
4oz (100 g) sugar
1 sponge cake – plain
17 fl oz (475 ml) whipped cream
3 apples peeled, sliced and lightly cooked so the pieces remain whole

First soak the gelatine in a little water (or follow packet instructions). Make up a custard by heating the milk and add chopped lemon balm. Leave to infuse for 15 minutes. Reheat and pour over beaten egg yolks and sugar. Return to heat and cook without boiling until it thickens. Strain, add gelatine and set aside to cool.

Line a terrine mould or cake tin with cling film and

then with thin slices of the sponge along the base and sides. When the custard is the same temperature as the cream, fold together. Half fill the terrine with the mix and then layer the apples onto the mix. Finally fill to the top, allowing enough room to seal with another layer of the sponge. Cover and chill for 3–4 hours. To serve, unmould onto a flat tray and slice. Serve with a lemon sauce or cream.

LEMON SAUCE

16 fl oz (450 ml) water
8 oz (225 g) sugar
juice of 4 lemons
zest of 1 lemon

Mix the ingredients and bring to the boil to dissolve the sugar. Serve.

Salads

A quiet revolution is happening to the salads of Britain thanks to people like Joy Larkcom who, in 1976, travelled around Europe on a horticultural scholarship investigating the salad plants of other countries. She collected a wide range of chicories and lettuces and persuaded a few brave seed growers in Britain (like Suffolk Herbs) to begin to offer these varieties. Now the curly leaf of Red Lollo lettuce, first introduced by Joy, is often served in restaurants and is even available in supermarkets.

Herb leaves for a salad can be divided into two groups. First, those herbs which, like lettuce, are used more for a crunchy, fresh texture than flavouring and therefore any amount can be used; such leaves are blanched dandelion, chicory and summer purslane which has a nutty flavour.

Second is the group of sharp-flavoured leaves which should be used only in small quantities as an accent. This would include leaves like basil, chives, lemon thyme, marjoram, mint, nasturtium, sorrel and salad rocket.

For the best flavour, pick at the last minute and only wash if necessary. Small leaves of basil, thyme and marjoram are best left whole while larger ones can be loosely chopped with a stainless steel knife or cut with scissors; tear large basil leaves.

The colourful range of herb leaves can be used to advantage in the presentation of salads. Gold variegated lemon balm can be spread through a green salad to give splashes of colour or a gradual colour change. To create the image of the opening of a giant flower place white chicory in the centre, an inner ring of bright green purslane and lemon balm, an outer ring of stripes of deep green sorrel and, outside, a row of purple salad bowl lettuce.

Flowers and roots are also returning to the salad arena and they are introduced in the flower and root chapters.

Teas

A drink to soothe, solace, heal, and cheer; teas made of aromatic leaves, flowers or roots steeped in water are the most ancient and popular liquid for our consumption. Many herbal tea leaves are easy to grow in our gardens and in addition can be calming and relaxing or stimulating and invigorating. Several herbal teas have specific therapeutic benefits and are used as treatments. Japanese research has discovered that green tea helps prevent stomach cancer.

The word tisane originally meant barley water from the Latin 'ptisana' and the Greek 'ptisane'. In the recent past it has been used to specify unfermented leaves as opposed to the fermented leaves of black tea. But here we use the term 'herb teas'.

It is written in the *Chinese Manual of the Origins of Customs* that the ceremony of offering tea to a guest began with Kwan Yin, the Goddess of Mercy, during the lifetime in which she was a disciple of Laotse. When he decided to depart to the western mountains she was first at the Han Pass and presented the 'Old Philosopher' with a cup of the golden elixir.

This is one of the most pleasurable aspects of tea, honouring friendship with a lovingly prepared simple drink and here we have much to learn from Eastern cultures.

Herbs can be used fresh or dried. As a rough guide, one part dried equals three parts fresh. Most herb teas are infused, that is, leaves or flowers are put into a warm teapot, boiling water is poured over and the tea is brewed for 3–5 minutes depending on the herb. One tsp (5 ml) of dried or 1 tbsp (15 ml) of fresh herbs is added for each cup of boiling water. Seeds and root are usually ground or pulversized in a pestle and mortar just before use and then made into a decoction; 1 tbsp (15 ml) of crushed root or seeds is put in 2 cups of boiling water and simmered until the water is reduced to 1 cup, approximately 5–20 minutes depending on the herb. Try mint, chamomile, linden, peppermint, rose hip and lemon verbena – as they are all easy to enjoy.

2
HERBAL FLOWERS

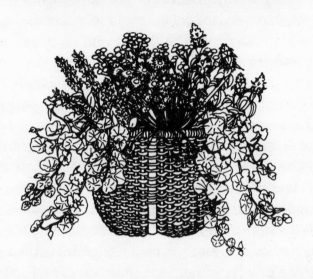

Flowers are the show stoppers of botany; the enchant-
ing, delicate, yet sensuous, pinnacle of a plant's beauty.
The flowers of herb plants have a special appeal. They are
generally soft colours and shapes flowering in abundance
with a blousey innocence that evokes images of old-
fashioned cottage gardens. Yet there are a few stunners
among them like the Madonna lily whose flowers were
once used to treat bruises and epilepsy.

There are flowers for eating in salads, soothing our
nerves, cleansing our skin and making fragrant gifts.
Among these, the world's favourite flower, the rose, offers
all these possibilities and is probably unsurpassed in its
range of herbal applications.

While the leaves of herbs provide the permanent

structure, colour and continuous pleasure of a herb garden, it is the flowers which, for a brief moment, can make our spirits soar. As the large flower bud of a tall graceful Madonna lily slowly swells, our anticipation grows until the pure-white, elegant petals unfold to assure us that this world is not mundane. The flower with its sweet, penetrating fragrance has been used as a pain killer and a cosmetic. The lily thrives on a sunny slope with good drainage. Unlike other lilies, the Madonna lily only roots from the base of the bulb so it requires just 2 in (5 cm) of soil above the bulb when planting and it shouldn't be allowed to dry out. Start with healthy stock and it will flourish undisturbed for many years. If you get the rich, yellow pollen of the lily on your clothes, you will also discover it is a strong dye.

Lavender is the essence of an English herb garden. Who could ever he without the silver leaves and soft purple flowers alight with white butterflies. It traditionally lines the pathway and promises sweet lavender bags to scent the winter months. To see whole fields of lavender in bloom is an unforgettable treat. It becomes one of those visions tucked in the mind to be called upon in troubled times.

The list of flowers with herbal uses is long indeed. The following are but a few: bergamot, sweet myrtle, marjoram and oregano, rosemary flowers, poppies, elderflower, primrose and cowslip, sage, daisy, nasturtium, mullein, rose, lavender, borage, calendula, chamomile, pyrethrum, chicory, clove pinks, meadowsweet, sweet woodruff, sweet rocket, hops, digitalis, skullcap, roses, violets, lupins, bugloss, musk mallow, goat's rue, jasmine, mock orange, lily, sweet clover, meadow crane's bill, peony and hound's tongue.

THEME GARDENS

In addition to their practical uses, the potent historical and romantic associations of herbal flowers make them a seductive theme for gardens.

Mary Gardens

The rose for pure love and martyrdom and the lily for purity and innocence are the emblems of Mary Gardens and plantings with these and other herbs associated with Mother Mary have been popular since earliest monastic days. There are medieval references to St Mary Gardens, walled and full of beautiful flowers and 'birds like angels'. At one point they reached near-cult proportions, to the concern of the Catholic hierarchy, and restrictive directives were issued. Many flowers carry the words 'Our Lady' in their name: Our Lady's mantle (*Aichemilla mollis*), Our Lady's smock (*Cardamine pratensis*), Our Lady's bedstraw (*Galium verum*), Our Lady's Garters (ribbon grass), though now the 'Our' is frequently dropped; lady's mantle, lady's smock, etc.

The blue of rosemary flowers is said to have been transformed from white when Mary laid her blue cloak over the plant. A legend relates that the white leaf veins of blessed milk thistle (*Silybum marianum*) came from Mary's milk. The name costamary (*Chrysanthemum balsamita* or *Tanacetum balsamita*), called Our Lady's balsam, comes from 'Costa' or 'kostos', the Greek name for a spicy

Oriental plant because of its spicy mint fragrance; and Mary because it was a plant of Mary or women in general. It was also called the Bible herb because early American Pilgrims carried the long, slender leaves as book-marks in their Bibles both to allay appetites during long sermons and as a long-lasting, green and fragrant bookmark. Forget-me-not, sometimes called 'Mary's eyes' and marigold (*Calendula officinalis*), once known as 'Marygold', claim Marian connections. Others include Our Lady's fingers (*Anthyllis vulneraria*), Our Lady's keys (cowslip), Our Lady's thimble (harebell), Our Lady's tears (lily-of-the-valley), Lady's orchid (*Orchis purpurea*), and Our Lady's tresses (*Spiranthes spiralis*). A combination of several of these herbs and wild flowers planted together as a Mary Garden could provide a gentle environment for quiet contemplation.

Herb Flowers in a Monastery Garden

The connection between religious orders and herb gardens is an ancient and honourable one. When the Romans came to Britain they introduced around 400 herbs: pot herbs, sweet herbs, salad herbs and their important medicinal plants. They also introduced the system of cultivating plants in enclosed gardens and the idea of a vegetable-medicine garden. When they left, only the hardiest herbs survived without the horticultural skills of the Roman gardeners. Many of the herbs were reintroduced during the Anglo-Saxon invasion of 449 AD and then by the monks who accompanied Augustine to Kent in 597 AD. Credit goes to the monks for restoring and maintaining the gardens of England and the herbs they contained through several bleak and troublesome centuries. They grew healing herbs in the physic garden and provided an area to sit and convalesce in the cloister garden. And in the Paradise gardens were the herbs and flowers for the altar to glorify God.

A monastery garden could include the widest range of herbs. It would also be the perfect place for a central, stone water fountain (the water of life), a vine-covered walkway, a bee hive and the statue of a beloved saint.

One can occasionally find a statue of Saint Fiacre, the patron saint of gardeners, St Francis of Assisi, or Clare of Assisi.

There are saints and holy beings associated with a love of nature, plants and healing in every spiritual movement. From Ancient Greece there is Asclepius, the God of Healing, and his three daughters: Hygieia, Goddess of Health; Iaso, whose name means 'to cure'; and Panacea, or 'all-healing'.

Two of my favourites are Kwan Yin and Lady Sengen Sama who is enshrined in a Shinto tablet at the foot of Mount Fuji. She represents the idea that simple, sensitive beauty is a powerful and permanent expression of higher truths and that a garden of peace, harmony and beauty is a focus of spiritual energy as worthy as any temple. What she embodies is encapsulated in the best of Japanese gardens.

There are many herbs mentioned in the Bible, the Koran, the Vedas and other Holy Books and many cultures have sacred plants such as the lotus, arum lily, mistletoe and vervain which could become the starting point or the focal point of a garden for contemplation.

A Garden of Shakespeare's Herbs

The diverse subjects encompassed by Shakespeare's eclectic knowledge included the herbs of his day and their uses and meaning. Over 80 culinary, medicinal and wild flower herbs are sprinkled through his poetry.

If you wanted to create a 'Shakespeare garden' it could include a knot garden using Shakespeare's 'winter herbs' with perhaps rosemary topiary. This herb can easily be clipped to a neat shape such as a sphere, column or cone, a popular feature of the time. The garden would have geometric paths and regular beds of herbs edged with the smaller evergreens like thyme and pinks. A central statue or fountain; seats; a bank of turf with small flowers growing among the grass, and an arbour or bower of fragrant plants would be suitable. This could be planted with honeysuckle and the several roses mentioned by Shakespeare (the white rose of York (*Rosa alba*) ; the red rose of Lancaster (*R. gallica officinalis*); the cabbage rose (*R. centifolia*); the damask rose (*R. trigentipetals*); rose of May (Cinnamon rose); the dog rose (*R. canina*), and the 'mingled' damask (*R. mundi*). The garden might be enclosed with a hedge of sweet briar or wattle fencing with rosemary against it. For an informal style to accommodate the wilder herbs mentioned by Shakespeare we can turn to the writings of Francis Bacon.

Bacon's essays include many modern ideas. He was concerned for health and freshness and dismissed a pond as unwholesome, 'full of flies and frogs', unless the water could be perpetually changed. He planned aromatic pockets of rosemary, wild strawberries and thyme and recommended walkways carpeted with sweet-scented herbs.

He also suggested an ancient Chinese garden idea, that of planting for enjoyment in all seasons, and recommended less familiar scents like the fragrance of wild strawberry leaves to scent the autumn air.

Fairie Herbs

In Shakespeare's time the fairies, elves, hobgoblins and sprites who flit through his plays were quite real to his contemporaries. The consensus was that their visible presence had been quite common in the past but that they no longer allowed themselves to be seen.

The writings of Shakespeare did much to change the image of fairies as mischievous, even frightening, creatures of the darkness to childlike creatures of the moonlight.

Herbs from Shakespeare's works associated with fairies and flowery meads include: forget-me-nots, lawn daisies (*Bellis perennis*), wild thyme, columbine, harebell, wild strawberry, cowslip, primrose, ox-eye daisy, lemon balm, yarrow, borage, saffron crocus, Adonis flower (*Anemone nemorosa*), salad burnet, clover, cuckoo-flowers (*Ranunculus varieties*), daffodils (small wild forms), pinks, fumitory (*Fumaria officinalis*), lady's smock, lark's heel (*Delphinium ajacis*), poppies, pansy, narcissus, mustard and Dian's bud (wormwood).

Sacred Herbs

There are nine herbs listed in an ancient Anglo-Saxon text, the *Lacnunga,* and there is a certain fascination in the belief that they could protect against physical, mental and emotional ailments. The herbs are chervil, crabapple, fennel, mugwort, maythen (chamomile), stime (water-cress), waybroed (plantain), wergula (nettle) and the previously unidentified atterlothe. It has now been trans-lated to cockspur grass by the Archaeological Unit in Bury St Edmunds and this is likely the 'Cock's head fitch' (Onobrychis), or sainfoin, of Culpeper's Herbal of 1645. This group of rather unruly and unattractive herbs could be given a bit of style by planting them with paths in the shape of a Celtic knot design with the crabapple tree in the centre.

The six herbs betony, vervain, peony root (named after Paeon, the physician of Olympus), plantain, yarrow and the rose were worn in an amulet to ward off evil and many sacred herbs were burned on hilltops on St John's Day (23 June). It was believed that they purified the air and protected people, livestock and crops. St John's wort was the best known.

HARVESTING FLOWERS

Flowers reach perfection and contain the highest propor-tion of active ingredients as they first open fully so this is the ideal time to pick them. Choose unblemished flowers of good shape as distorted flowers can indicate damage from pests, chemical sprays or a virus. They are best collected at midday in dry weather and it is easiest to pick the whole flowering stem and separate the flowers later indoors, free from wind. If you pick flower-heads, try to avoid touching the petals. Keep them loose in open containers as they bruise easily and soon begin to sweat. Cut flowering stems of lavender and thyme just as the flowers open.

When picking for culinary use, check for insects and dirt and find out if the area has been sprayed with chemicals. Look inside the tube of bergamot flowers as it is an ideal home for small creepy-crawlies. Avoid flowers which will need washing as this will spoil the texture. Very few petals are poisonous; even the daffodil, whose bulb has killed people when mistakenly cooked for an onion, has an edible flower. But of the poisonous plants it is safest to assume that the poisonous principles are also in the flowers so do not eat the following:

Poisonous Plants

Alder buckthorn (*Frangula alnus*)
Baneberry (*Actaea spicata*)
Bittersweet (*Solanum dulcamara*)
Black nightshade (*Solanum nigrum*)
Buckthorn (*Rhamnus cathartica*)
Bryony black (*Tamus communis*)
Bryony white (*Bryonia dioica*)
Buttercup family (*Ranunculus*)
Columbine (*Aquilegia vulgaris*)
Cowbane (*Cicuta virosa*)
Daphne (*Daphne mezereum*)
Darnel rye grass (*Lolium temulentum*)
Deadly nightshade (*Atropa bella-donna*)
Dog's mercury (*Mercurialis perennis*)
Fool's parsley (*Aethusa cynapium*)
Foxglove (*Digitalis purpurea*)
Fritillary (*Fritillaria meleagris*)
Green hellebore (*Helleborus viridis*)
Stinking hellebore (*Helleborus foetidus*)

Hemlock (*Conium maculatum*)
Henbane (*Hyoscyamus niger*)
Ivy (*Hedera helix*)
Laburnum – all varieties
Lily-of-the-valley (*Convallaria majalis*)
Meadow saffron (*Colchicum autumnale*)
Mistletoe (*Viscum album*)
Monkshood (*Aconitum napellus*)
Privet (*Ligustrum vulgare*)
Spindle tree (*Euonymus europaeus*)
Spurges, all (*Euphorbia*)
Spurge-laurel (*Daphne laureola*)
Thorn apple (*Datura stramonium*)
Yew (*Taxus baccata*)

When picking just a few flowers for immediate use, separate them from the calyx, the green backing of the flower which is attached to the stem, as you pick them. With borage, if you hold the flower by the black anthers and twist gently, the whole flower will part from the calyx leaving you with that extraordinarily beautiful blue star in your hand.

The flower part used most often in herbal recipes is the petal. The green sepals, or calyx, is usually removed as it has a bitter taste. For rose petals, other large petals and any with green shading at the base, tear off the bottom section as it may be bitter. For daisy-type flowers, and any with hard centres, pull off their petals and sprinkle them on at the last minute. Small flowers like thyme and marjoram can be left whole.

DRYING FLOWERS

Petals like calendula and roses, and all the flowers for pot pourri, should be dried in a dust-free environment with good ventilation out of direct sunlight. This is usually done by laying petals or whole, small flowers on gauze stretched over a frame so that the air can circulate. At a pinch, they can be laid on newspaper but then they need to be turned occasionally. Make sure the petals do not overlap as they may not dry properly. The ideal temperature for the first day is 90°F (32°C), then 75–80°F (24–28°C) afterwards. Allow four to seven days for small flowers and up to two or three weeks for thick petals. Small rose buds and the thick petals of lilies will need turning once or twice.

Several flowers such as lavender, chamomile, delphiniums, larkspur, love-in-a-mist and the everlasting flowers can be dried on the stem. Either lay the flowering stems on open trays or hang them upside down in small bunches, not more than ten stems together.

If only the lavender flowers are required, say for sweet bags or recipes, they can be rubbed off when needed but don't discard the stems. Burn them on an open fire for fragrance or make incense by soaking them with 1 tbsp dissolved saltpetre for 30 minutes.

The same drying procedure is used for medicinal and cosmetic recipes. The best quality is necessary for medical, culinary and tea herbs and each variety should be dried separately so that confusion does not arise. Cleanliness must be a priority during drying and storage.

Finally, store the flowers in dark jars or paper bags, with the name and date. Those required for decoration need to be stored flat in a rigid container.

Freezing Flowers

Borage and sweet violet flowers can be captured in an ice-cube to be used as a garnish for cool drinks. Place violets face down and borage flowers with their black anthers upward in the base of an ice-cube container. This way you will see the face of the violet but avoid the black bits of the borage sticking out and looking like a dead fly in your drink. Gently add water to cover and freeze. If you have difficulty keeping the flower in position, just put a little water on the top, freeze and then fill the cube and freeze again.

COSMETIC USES

Flower Waters

Four flower waters have become classic skin tonics as their reputation after hundreds of years of use has not diminished. Lavender water is suitable for delicate and sensitive skins; it is very healing as it speeds cell replacement and is mildly antiseptic to help reduce acne. Orange flower water also has a reputation for stimulating the replacement of old cells; it helps in the treatment of dry skin and broken capillaries and is said to help restore the skin's acid balance. Rose water is a tonic for dry, sensitive and mature skins with a refining and softening effect. Elderflower is good for mature or sallow skins; it softens the texture, helps to smooth wrinkles and fades freckles. It, too, has healing properties and is soothing for sunburn.

The flower waters can be used as they are as an astringent or refresher, or they can be mixed with other ingredients for additional benefits such as the following rosewater tonic recipe. Mix 2 parts rosewater with 1 part witch hazel and a few drops of glycerine for its softening properties. It includes distilled witch hazel, made from the leaves and bark of the shrub and is astringent and soothing. The witch hazel from the chemist contains 15 per cent alcohol which means it will keep almost indefinitely. When it is mixed with a water-based liquid the percentage of alcohol is diluted and the preservative qualities with it.

Flower Astringents

Cornflowers and meadowsweet flowers have astringent properties and an infusion makes an effective refresher.

generous handful of cornflowers or meadowsweet
flowers
½ pt (300 ml) boiling water
1 tsp (5 ml) witch hazel

Infuse flowers and water and allow to cool. Strain, add witch hazel, bottle and keep refrigerated.

Cornflowers and meadowsweet can also be used in a cleansing milk along with gentle chamomile to soften and lighten the skin (excellent for under-eye shadows). Lime blossom soothes and softens and has a reputation for deep cleansing, and sweet violets have a gentle soothing astringent action. They can be used individually or blended.

Three Flower Cleansing Milk

½ cup (125 ml) buttermilk
1 tbsp (15 ml) chamomile flowers
1 tbsp (15 ml) lime blossom
1 tbsp (15 ml) elder blossom

Put all the ingredients in a double boiler, and simmer for 30 minutes. Do not allow the milk to boil. Leave to infuse and cool and for a further two hours and strain. Store in the refrigerator and use within a week. Apply with cotton wool and tissue off. Follow with a skin tonic.

Cowslip Cleanser

Cowslip flowers are said to aid deep cleansing, clearing the skin of dirt and perspiration.

small handful of cowslip flowers and stalks
½ pt (300 ml) boiling water
2 tsp (10 ml) witch hazel

Infuse flowers until cool, strain; add witch hazel and use as a cleanser.

Bath Flowers

Tie a handful of flowers in a muslin bag and hang this under your running water as you draw a bath.

Relaxing bath herbal flowers: chamomile, jasmine, lime flowers, meadowsweet
Deep cleansing bath herbal flowers: rose petals
Healing bath herbal flowers (for sunburn or wind burn):

calendula, red clover, lavender
Tranquilizing herbal flowers: chamomile, cowslips, jasmine, lavender, lime blossom, mullein, violets
Sauna herbal flowers: rose petals, lavender.

HOUSEHOLD USES

Lavender

The unique, fresh, spicy scent of lavender with its echoes of cleanliness and purity is enjoyed by men and women alike. Among all scents it comes closest to encapsulating the caring and comforting qualities of home.

The name lavender derives from the Latin lavare, 'to wash' and, indeed, its fresh clean scent was the favourite bath water addition of the Greeks and Romans. The laundry man in Edward VI's court manual *The Black Book* was called the lavender man and he was authorized to procure 'sufficient whyte soap tenderly to wasshe the stuffe from the King's propyr person'.

In warm climates, like that of southern Italy where the sun draws the fragrance of the flowers into the air, housewives drape their laundry over bushes of lavender and rosemary to perfume the clothes as they are drying.

It was a popular strewing herb both for its insect-repelling properties and its long-lasting fragrance. Today these qualities are still valued and lavender bags or bundles are tucked into drawers, under pillows, in linen shelves and stored with special garments like a wedding dress. Charles VI of France had lavender-filled white satin cushions to lounge upon.

To make a lavender bundle, use fresh lavender as the

dried stalks will not bend to create the shape. However, once made they will keep well. A mature plant can provide 1000 spikes.

On a dry day, pick an odd number (usually between 9 and 15 depending on their bulkiness) of well-formed lavender stalks with plump flowers just opened. Strip off their leaves, line up the base of the flower heads and cut the stalks to a uniform length. Select a 3 ft (1 m) piece of ¼ in (6 mm) wide ribbon in a sympathetic colour like mauve or blue. Leave an 8-in (20-cm) tail of ribbon and tie it around the bundle just below the heads. Bend back each of the heads gently to create a cage over the stems. Pull the long piece of ribbon through the outside and weave it in and out of the flower heads in a continuous spiral until the end of the heads is reached. Tie a bow together with the short end of ribbon and either make a loop to hang it by or tie it again at the end of the stalks. The ribbon helps contain the individual flowers if they drop off their stem as they dry.

DECORATIVE AND AROMATIC USES

Pot Pourri

A favourite way of capturing the bounty of the summer herb garden to enjoy through the year is to make pot pourri. This is a colourful, dried mixture of sweet-scented flowers and aromatic leaves. Roses and lavender are the first choice of flower ingredients as they keep their scent for the longest time. Other fragrant flowers are acacia, broom, carnation, elder, freesia, honeysuckle, hyacinth, jasmine, lilac, lily-of-the-valley, linden or lime blossom, meadowsweet, orange blossom and Mexican orange blossom, mignonette, mock orange, narcissus, nicotiana, stock, sweet rocket, violet and wallflower.

To prepare flowers for pot pourri follow the instructions for drying them on p. 75.

Some flowers are selected for their colour, especially in the blue range, and aromatic leaves make up the remainder of the body of a pot pourri. These often have a stronger or sharper aroma than flowers so they should be chosen carefully to blend with the flowers you have selected. Dry them whole and then crush or crumble them to release their scent. Leave a few whole for a change of scale.

When making your own pot pourri, select from: alecost, balm of Gilead, balsam poplar buds, basil, bay, bearberry, bergamot, lady's bedstraw, lemon balm, lemon verbena, melilot, mints (spearmint, apple, peppermint and especially eau-de-cologne), patchouli, pelargoniums, (rose, lemon, apple, orange, pine, nutmeg and peppermint), rosemary, sage (especially pineapple), southernwood, sweet briar, sweet majoram, sweet myrtle, sweet cicely, tarragon, thymes (lemon and pine), wild strawberry and woodruff.

After leaves and flowers, the third group is spices. Spices, aromatic roots and peel give extra depth and lasting qualities to a pot pourri blend. Again, freshly crush or grind spices in a pestle and mortar and grate nutmeg to release the aroma, but leave a few whole for textural interest. Try alexander seed, allspice, aniseed, cardamom, cinnamon, cloves, coriander, dill seed, ginger, juniper, nutmeg, star anise and vanilla pods.

Roots should be cleaned, peeled, sliced and slowly dried. Then chop, crush or powder them to the desired size. Use the aromatic roots of angelica, elecampane, sweet-flag, valerian, cowslip and vetiver (*Vetiveria zizanioides*).

To dry your own peel, take a thin layer of peel with a zester, grater or potato peeler, avoiding any white pith. Dip in orris powder to intensify the scent. Dry slowly, then crush or mince if desired. Use the peel of orange, lemon, lime, bergamot and tangerine.

Wood rasping are particularly exciting to work with as some of their scents are quite new and unusual. Choose from shreds or raspings of cedarwood, rosewood, sandal-wood, cassia chips and any of the fruit woods like apple, pear or cherry which have a faint but sweet aroma, and look out for new varieties available. If you discover any-thing unusual it is worth checking from the supplier if the wood has any skin irritating properties. The highly concentrated essential oils of cassia, cinnamon bark, dwarf pine, thuja, and wintergreen are toxic and should never be applied to skins, though the wood chippings, as far as we know, do not irritate the skin when they are handled.

All spices have a strong aroma and should be used sparingly. The ideal quantity is about 1 tbsp (15 ml) to 4 cups of flowers and leaves. Selected spices are usually added in equal proportions. These can give a 'musky' or 'oriental' quality, or suggest a 'masculine' or 'winter' scent.

The final ingredient for a pot pourri is a fixative. This is an aromatic plant part which gives up its fragrance very slowly and thereby lasts longer. In perfume blending it is called a basenote. As the odiferous molecules evaporate more slowly, they slow down the evaporation rate of other scents present, hence they all last longer.

There are various vegetable fixatives. One is orris root from *Iris florentina* (the most popular as its sweet violet scent doesn't strongly affect a blend); use approximately 1 tbsp (15 ml) per cup of flowers and leaves. Gum benzoin from *Strayx benzoin,* called 'oil of ben' or 'benjamin' in old recipes, has a sweet aromatic scent, a little like vanilla; use about ½ oz (15 gm) to 4–6 cups of flowers and leaves. Tonka bean from *Dipterix odorata* has a strong vanilla scent; use one or two beans per recipe. Storax is from *Liquidamber orientalis;* use as gum benzoin.

A few fragrances double as fixatives and this useful group includes sweet flag root, sweet violet root, sandalwood, patchouli, vetiver (mentioned above) and also frankincense and myrrh (available as oils or resin), and oakmoss. Oakmoss from *Evernia pranastri* is sometimes called chypre or cypre, a name now applied to a group of perfume blends. Use ½ oz (15 gm) to 4 cups of flowers and leaves. Orris and sweet flag can be grown in a temperate climate but purchase the other ingredients from a herb shop.

When you have assembled your ingredients, like the mistress of the 'still room' in Elizabethan times, take a moment to linger over the scent and colour of each flower and leaf. Scented flowers traditionally dominate a pot pourri blend. Choose a theme to harmonize your mixture; say cottage flowers, a woodland blend of musky scents, a fresh mint and citrus blend or a mixture of soothing herbs such as rose petals, lavender, lemon verbena, meadowsweet and chamomile. It is a pleasurable task to educate one's nose to the blending of sweet scents.

Several of the flower, leaf and spice ingredients are available as essential oils and a single drop is a powerful perfume. These can be used with discretion to strengthen a blend or revive a flagging mixture. (Pot pourri boosters for sale are a mixture of real or synthetic essential oils in a carrier such as alcohol.) In the beginning, the temptation is to use too much. So experiment with a few drops first after you have mixed your blend of flowers, leaves and spices, adding it drop by drop and stirring it in between. Put the mixture away in a sealed container in a warm, dry area for six weeks to cure.

When the pot pourri is ready, display it in an open bowl where it can be fingered to release further fragrance and consider the colour and decoration of your containers so they harmonize with the colours and theme of your mixture.

Summer Herb Garden Pot Pourri

Using dried flowers and leaves, the following is a suggested guide to combinations and quantities.

flowers for scent:

   2 cups rose petals
   1 cup rose buds
   2 cups lavender
   1 cup clove pinks
   ½ cup sweet violets

leaves for scent:
    ½ cup rosemary
    ½ cup sweet myrtle
    ½ cup bergamot
    ½ cup eau-de-cologne mint
    ¼ cup bay
    ¼ cup southernwood

flowers for colour:
    ½ cup bergamot
    ¼ cup calendula petals
    ¼ cup borage or forget-me-not
    ¼ cup deep blue delphinium
    ¼ cup feverfew flowers
    3 Madonna lily whole or separated
    into petals as an accent

spices:
    1 tbsp (15 ml) ground cloves
    1 tbsp (15 ml) ground allspice

fixative:
    5 tbsp (75 ml) orris root

Decorated Writing Paper

First dry flowers by pressing them between sheets of blotting paper or newsprint set between heavy books. Suitable flowers would be primrose, sweet violet, borage, daisy, gypsophila and forget-me-not, or unusual shapes such as salad burnet, chervil, pelargonium, alpine lady's mantle or sprigs of rosemary, lemon thyme, patchouli and myrtle. When they are thoroughly dried, use a small amount of latex-based glue to fix the herbs to greeting cards, book marks, place cards, tallies, invitations and parcels. When arranging the leaves or sprigs on a surface take into account their natural patterns of growth and try to reflect the elegant curve of a stem or the shy emergence of a flower.

Scented Writing Paper

This is achieved by storing paper with scented herbs in an enclosed space to allow the paper to absorb the fragrance. Place quantities of aromatic dried leaves or lavender flowers, or drops of essential oil between sheets of writing paper in a closed box. Leave for six weeks to absorb the fragrance.

Drawer Lining Paper

The textured back of wallpaper absorbs scent well and can be used to line drawers. Lay thin muslin bags of aromatic herbs and essential oil between layers of lining paper. Roll them up into one cylinder shape and wrap them in cling film for six weeks.

Colour Inks

For red ink, collect 1 cup full of field poppy petals. Pour on a minimum amount of boiling water to cover and steep overnight. Add 15 per cent isopropyl alcohol or vodka to preserve the solution. Strain and bottle. A pale blue ink can be made from cornflowers.

USING FLOWERS IN THE GARDEN

Pyrethrum Insecticide

The herb flower pyrethrum, *Chrysanthemum cinerariifolium,* contains a natural insecticide that is non-toxic to mammals so it can be used to treat pests on the skin of humans and animals, as well as plants. It is non-cumulative and decomposes rapidly. The flowers can be dried and powdered to sprinkle on plants which has some effect but better results are obtained from making a spray. When dealing with pyrethrum flowers, do wear gloves as prolonged contact may cause skin allergies.

To make a spray, the powder must first be steeped in an alcohol, like methylated spirits, and then diluted with water. The active ingredient does not dissolve properly in water. Soak 2 oz (50 g) of powdered pyrethrum flowers in 3 fl oz (75 ml) methylated spirit. Dilute with 6 gals (27 l) water and spray on plants. Keep in a dark container and use quickly as it may deteriorate in the presence of sunlight.

The solution paralyses ants, aphids, bedbugs, cockroaches, flies, mosquitoes and spider mites. Unfortunately it also kills helpful insects and began its life as a fish poison in Malaysia so it shouldn't be used near fish ponds. If you spray pyrethrum at dusk, bees will be safe by morning when they begin working. An extra note: if the active ingredients pyrethin or cinerin are extracted from the flower and therefore concentrated, they *are* toxic to humans and animals so check the labels carefully if you buy it prepared.

Honey Bee Garden

Bees are useful in our gardens because they fertilize the fruit, flowers and vegetables giving us ripe fruit and viable seeds and, of course, somewhere they are making honey and royal jelly.

The flowers of herbs are particularly attractive to bees as many are still the original species with single flowers (not hybridized to create layers of petals which are more difficult for bees to work). Favourites are the Labiatae or lavender family which includes the often aromatic two-lipped flowers such as ajuga, basil, bergamot, hyssop, lavender, lemon balm, mints, marjoram, oregano, rose-mary, sage, savories and thyme.

Bees also enjoy the normally blue, five-petalled flowers of the Boragineae family like borage, forget-me-not, comfrey and lungwort. They also work the five-petalled flowers of the Malaceae or mallow family which includes hollyhock, marsh mallow, musk mallow, tree mallow and the rose of Sharon.

A few extra considerations make every herb garden safer and more useful for these pollinating insects. A garden specially for bees should be in full sunlight for maximum nectar production with the herbs grown in groups of five or more. A surrounding hedge or fence helps prevent the wind from buffeting the bees. A hedge of holly mixed with ivy is ideal as the holly supplies nectar in late spring and the ivy in autumn. Yew produces some pollen in early spring while cherry-laurel gives nectar in mid-spring and also produces a sweet fluid on the underside of its leaves which is valuable to hive bees when nectar is scarce. Clovers, lime and fruit trees, oil-seed rape, sainfoin, mustard, charlock, willow herb and dandelion are the most important nectar plants for bees. Try to select herbs to provide nectar and pollen for the longest possible period.

Bumble Bee Garden

The honey bee garden also creates an opportunity to aid our dwindling population of bumble bees. These large, furry, gentle bees begin foraging several weeks earlier than the honey bee and being working earlier in the day often continuing through wind and rain. The familiar buzzing is not produced by the 200 beats per second of the wings but rather by the passage of air through many tiny air holes in the bee's thorax supplying extra oxygen for flight fuel. Several species have already become extinct and more are in danger because their hibernating sites and sources of early nectar (mainly willows) occur on wet lands which vanish as agricultural land is drained.

Try to include a pussy-willow (Salix ssp) somewhere in your garden and plenty of the early spring-flowering deadnettle varieties for early nectar. Bumble bees will obtain nectar from the same plants as honey bees but in addition they work flowers with longer corollas as the bumble bees have a longer probiscis or drinking tube. Lemon balm and bergamot are in this category as well as aquilegia, comfrey, foxglove, honeysuckle, lilac, lupin, nasturtium and wood sage.

MEDICINAL FLOWERS

Cold Remedies

Elderflower is excellent in a cold remedy, especially mixed

with yarrow and peppermint leaves (see p. 57) and an infusion will help cure a sore throat.

An infusion of ½ oz [15 g] elderflowers and ½ oz [15 g] lime blossom in 1 pt [600 ml] boiling water for 15 minutes will also treat a cold. Take a cupful 3 times a day.

Calendula Cream

Calendula is used to make a healing ointment for rough and cracked skin. Make an infused oil of calendula petals, following the instructions on p. 30, repeating with fresh petals several times to increase the potency. Then melt 1 oz (25 g) beeswax, and blend with 4 fl oz (100 ml) of the warmed herbal oil. Add another 1 oz (25 g) of calendula petals and simmer gently for ten minutes, stirring frequently. Strain through double muslin into a wide-necked jar. Stir in a drop of tincture of myrrh or benzoin to extend its life. Don't use borax as it can damage broken skin. Label and date.

A cooled decoction of calendula can be used to soothe burns and a hot poultice to treat bruises. The flower can be crushed and applied to a sting or rubbed on an insect bite for relief.

Floral Infusions

An infusion of lime blossom, chamomile or lavender flowers will also help treat insomnia. Take 1 cup at night before retiring. An infusion of chamomile can also relieve toothache, if repeatedly used to rinse the mouth.

Poisonous Medical Flowers

Foxglove (*Digitalis purpurea*) has provided the primary

heart drug for over 200 years and though the main ingredient has been synthesized, the plant is still grown commercially for the pharmaceutical industry. Foxgloves are poisonous and should not be used domestically.

All parts of the opium poppy (*Papaver somniferum*), except the ripe seeds, are dangerous, and should only be used by trained medical personnel.

Poppies have always been considered significant because of their narcotic effect. The opium poppy was a cult plant of the Sumerians 5000 years ago. The name 'somniferum' means 'sleep inducing' and 'opus' is from the Greek for juice. It was one of the first to be investigated with scientific apparatus and represents a turning point in the transition from the magic and religious use of plants to scientific analysis. It also examples the benefits and dangers of reducing plants to chemical components. Morphine and codeine were extracted, providing our most important pain killers, but also heroin, whose side effect outweighs its value. Heroin is in the most toxic class of poisons (super toxic, class 6) and when you read the other members of the group you get a glimpse of what a body taking heroin would have to cope with. The super toxic 'class-mates' include cyanide, strychnine and nicotine.

The opium latex scraped from the green seed capsules was used to relieve pain, diarrhoea and some coughs but now it is mainly grown as a source of morphine.

CULINARY USES

Flower cuisine is the celebration of the most beautiful parts of the garden with the skill and pleasure of the kitchen. The very phrase 'edible flowers' conjures up exotic sensory delights, and cooking with flowers is an ancient skill in many countries. Jasmine, peonies and lotus, for example, make their way into an array of oriental dishes. The Chinese use the small garland chrysanthemum (C. coronarium) in soups, as a garnish and fry it in batter. Another chrysanthemum (C. indicum) is considered a valuable tonic useful to include with 'medicinal meals' and it is part of the Taoist elixir of immortality. Teas are flavoured with osmanthus and jasmine flowers, while lotus and lily buds can be found in soups and delicate savoury dishes.

In Persia and India, the rose has been used to garnish and flavour food for thousands of years. It is mentioned in the first-century Greek cookbook *Banquets for the Learned*. In Arabic countries, the rose is used to flavour every type of dish from soups and savoury courses cooked with dried rose buds, to honey-layered pastries and Turkish delight. Orange flower water from the orange blossom is also used throughout the Middle East in a wide range of delicately flavoured dishes.

But flowers are not alien to the kitchens of Britain. There is a recipe for Saracen sauce which includes roses in the earliest-known English cookbook written in the late fourteenth century by the chefs of Richard II. Salad flowers were popular for centuries and there are old recipes for flowers in soups and sauces, tarts and puddings, and jams and conserves. Pinks in drinks, elderflower champagne and cowslip wine are ancient favourites. Lavender was used to flavour conserves, make lavender vinegar and lavender wine. In 1573, Thomas Tusser in his planting list of 'Seeds and Herbs for the Kitchen' included 'saffron, marigold, primrose and violets of all sorts. '

The flowers of pungent-leaved herbs often have a milder version of the leaves' flavour. Nasturtium, mustard, mint, salad rocket and chive flowers come into this category while sage, thyme and rosemary flowers have a delicate hint of their leaf scent. If rosemary flowers are pounded into sugar and left for a few days, they will impart a light spicyness that goes well with fruit desserts like fools and creams. Calendula, too, has a mild flavour while pinks, roses and sweet violets radiate a little of the perfume for which each is famous. Others, like borage, pansies, daisy petals and mallows, are used more for their unusual colour and texture than their flavour.

Lavender is very strongly flavoured and only tiny amounts are used, sprinkled sparingly as you might use pepper. It is found in some *Herbs de Provence* mixtures which are prepared for casseroles and stews. This mixture usually includes dried thyme, rosemary, marjoram, savory, oregano, basil, tarragon and a small amount of lavender which gives a light, spicy perfume to the traditional savoury herbs.

Flowers in the Preparation of Salad

Choose when in season from anchusa, basil, bergamot petals, borage, broom (in small quantities only as vast amounts can be toxic), calendula, chicory, common chives and Chinese chives, cowslip, forget-me-nots, garland chrysanthemum (*Chrysanthemum coronarium*), violet, hollyhock petals and flower buds, hounds tongue flowers, lavender (sparingly), lawn daisy (*Bellis perennis*), mallow petals (marsh mallow, musk mallow and tree mallow), marjoram flowers, meadow cranes bill, mint florets (surprisingly pleasant), mustard, nasturtium, pansies, pelargonium, petunia petals, primrose, rose petals, rosemary flowers, sage flowers, salad rocket flowers, salsify, scorzonera, sweet rocket, sweet violet, thyme flowers, verbascum petals and viper's bugloss flowers. Yellow toadflax has an interesting taste rather like a raw courgette.

Some flowers which I have tried that I wouldn't recommend are: single pinks (*D. deltoides*) which are quite bitter; wall germander, wood betony and goat's rue flowers are also a little bitter; clary sage (too sharp for my taste); hyssop, which has an unexpected sweet perfume when the nectar is at maximum production. But there is then a bitter aftertaste.

There is no hard and fast rule to be applied to the art of salad making. Rather, the best approach is to cast an eye over the salad counter of your local supermarket, market stalls or your own garden and by so doing you will soon become aware of the items with the greatest appeal, *i.e.* colour, freshness, originality, etc.

It is best to combine flowers with a basic conventional background of salad leaves as the flower heads are appreciated better when they are not just jumbled together.

When assembling such salads, handle everything as lightly as possible, washing the leaves only when absolutely necessary and making sure they are dry by tossing or swinging them in a dry tea cloth.

Vinaigrette sauces should complement as far as possible the texture and flavour of a salad. Remember to be sparing with the vinegar, as salads are often ruined by the sharp shock of the heavy-handed addition of vinegar. Perhaps you could try a few drops of a flower vinegar.

CRYSTALLIZED FLOWERS

Single petals rather than whole flowers look more elegant, as unless extremely carefully done, the frosting tends to destroy the delicacy of the bloom.

In the case of flower heads, such as elder, which are extremely fragile, it is best to leave them intact, and then gently break off little florets after frosting.

1 egg white
castor sugar

Whisk up the egg white enough to break up the albumen but not as stiffly as for a meringue. Paint the petals using a small paint brush.

Pour a good layer of castor sugar onto a large plate and dip the petals into the sugar. Take care to cover completely as the sugar acts as the preservative. Spread some grease-proof paper on a tray and lay out the petals carefully. Leave for several hours before use, preferably in an airing cupboard or boiler room.

The excess sugar can be re-used in cakes or puddings.

If dried carefully after the frosting process, petals and flowers will keep a reasonable length of time stored between layers of grease-proof paper in a lidded container.

Flower Vinegars

To make floral vinegars follow the recipe on p. 31 with a light wine vinegar using any of the perfumed flowers.

Choose from broom, clover, elderflower, lavender, nasturtiums, clove-scented pinks, rose petals or sweet violets. Sweet-scented floral vinegars are used in special salad dressings, fruit dishes and certain meat dishes cooked with fruits. Some are suitable in cosmetic recipes.

Pickled Flowers

Flowers can be preserved for use in salads or meat dishes by pickling them, although some colour is leached out by the vinegar. Place a layer of flowers in the base of your pickle jar, sprinkle with sugar to cover, repeat flower and sugar layers until jar is filled, compacting them firmly. Boil and cool cider or wine vinegar and cover the layers. Seal and set aside for at least four days to allow flavours to mingle. Try this with calendula, chicory, salsify and scorzonera flowers and rosebuds and broom buds as well as the cowslips, elder and pinks which John Evelyn recommends.

Picnic Dishes

CHERRY AND ROSE PETAL SOUP (Serves 6–8)
1 good, fragrant rose bloom – pink or red
4 oz (100 g) demerara sugar
large pinch powdered cinnamon
1 pt (600 ml) cold water
1 lb (450 g) fresh stoned cherries (or drained, tinned cherries)
8 fl oz (225 ml) medium-dry white wine
1 tbsp (15 ml) Kirsch
½ pt (300 ml) soured cream

Remove rose petals from the flower head and cut away their bitter white heels. Reserve a few of the smallest and prettiest for decoration.

Combine sugar, cinnamon and water, bring to the boil and add the cherries. Simmer fresh cherries for about ½ hour (tinned cherries for 10 minutes). Add the white wine and the rose petals – not forgetting to leave some for decoration – and allow to stand until cool.

Liquidize or process the soup, then stir in the Kirsch and half the soured cream. Place in the refrigerator to chill thoroughly.

Serve either in a large glass bowl or individual glass dishes. Trickle a swirl of cream on top and scatter with a few rose petals.

CORIANDER AND CALENDULA QUICHE (Serves 6)

Pastry
(to line an 8-in [20-cm] flan or quiche tin with removable base)
6 oz (175 g) plain flour
large pinch of salt
3 oz (75 g) unsalted butter (or margarine and butter mixed)
1 egg yolk
1 tbsp (15 ml) cold water

Sift flour and salt. Cut cooking fat into small cubes then rub into the flour until the mixture looks like fine breadcrumbs. Sprinkle the egg yolk beaten with the cold water over the flour. Using a table knife, cut and stir to bring the mixture together until it leaves the side of the bowl fairly clean.

Gather together with the hands and rest the pastry for 20 minutes in a cool place before rolling.

In the meantime, switch on the oven set at 350°F (190°C) Mark 4. Grease the pastry tin and lightly dust with flour.

Roll out the pastry and line the tin, making sure that you do not stretch the pastry as you do this – the pastry will shrink back during cooking if it is badly handled. Prick the base all over with a fork.

Line the pastry case with grease-proof paper and weight down with dry beans or pebbles. Bake for 15 minutes in the centre of the oven, then remove the lining, turn down the oven to 325°F (170°C) Mark 3, and place the pastry on the lowest shelf of the oven for a further 5 minutes. This allows the base to dry out a little without risk of over browning.

Remove from oven and allow to cool before filling.

Savoury Custard Filling
  2 oz (50 g) grated Gruyère cheese (or a good dry Cheddar)
  ½ pt (300 ml) single cream
  2 large whole eggs
  1 egg yolk
  petals of 1 large calendula flower
  2 tbsp (30 ml) chopped coriander leaves
  salt and freshly ground white pepper

Cover the base of the cooked pastry with grated cheese.

Stir beaten eggs into the cream and season. (Do not over-beat the eggs as it spoils the smooth texture of the custard.) Stir in calendula petals and chopped coriander leaves, then gently pour the mixture over the cheese in the pastry shell.

Bake for 35–40 minutes. The top should be set, slightly risen and light brown.

Try to serve straight from the oven as the textures are at their very best when the tart is warm. It is, of course, quite delicious cold.

ROSE LAYERED DESSERT

1 cup loosely-packed, scented rose petals, white heels removed
4 mashed bananas
approx 4 oz (100 g) chopped dates (quantity to equal volume of mashed bananas)
2 tbsp (30 ml) mincemeat
4 tbsp (60 ml) rose petal jam*
juice of 2 oranges
¼ pt (150 ml) double cream

Cover a dish with rose petals – pink and red, preferably. Mix the bananas, dates and mincemeat and make a layer over the petals leaving the petals protruding around the edge. Cover with a layer of rose petal jam.

When ready to serve, pour the orange juice over the top. Add a layer of whipped cream and garnish with crystallized rose petals.

*Rose petal jam is available from good herbalist stores, but it is quite possible to use apple jelly instead.

GOOSEBERRY AND ELDERFLOWER COMPOTE

1 lb (450 g) gooseberries topped and tailed
4 oz (100 g) light muscovado sugar
2 clean heads of elderflower

Place gooseberries and sugar in a heavy saucepan, lay the elderflower heads on the top. Cover the pan and simmer gently until the fruit has softened and almost collapsed. Shake from time to time to prevent sticking. Allow the fruit to cool completely before removing the flower heads.

The fruit can be served just like this as delicious compote, but a little more effort can transform it into a creamy fool or an ice-cream.

GOOSEBERRY FOOL

Stir into the gooseberries two beaten eggs and ½ pt (300 ml) of double cream. Warm gently, stirring continuously, until the mixture thickens. Pour into dishes and garnish with florets of frosted elderflowers.

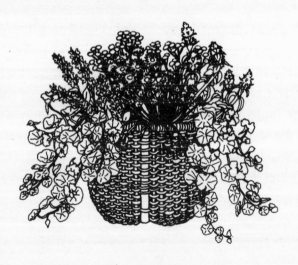

CREAM HEARTS SCENTED WITH SWEET GERANIUM LEAVES

Perforated porcelain dishes from France, used for draining the cream mixture, are available in England, but not easily found. It is perfectly possible to use empty yogurt or cream cheese cartons with a few holes punched in the bottom – or why not a flower pot?

Do be sure to dampen the muslin (or handkerchieves) before lining as it clings nicely to the shape of the dishes.

1 pt (600 ml) double cream
4 oz (100 g) curd cheese
2 egg whites
8 small, sweet geranium leaves
8 sweet geranium flowers
8 squares of muslin

Combine the cream and the cheese as thoroughly as possible. Whip the egg whites until they are softly peaked but not too dry. If you have a sweet tooth, add just a suggestion of sugar, but it is best left without. Fold egg whites into the cream.

Line your dishes or pots with dampened squares of muslin. Place a small geranium leaf at the bottom of each dish (over the muslin) and spoon in the cream mixture carefully, making sure that all the corners are well-filled. Place dishes on a rack over a plastic tray to drain in the cool. Leave for at least 8 hours.

About an hour before serving, turn out carefully and arrange prettily on a large plate. Decorate each cream with a sweet geranium flower and garnish the plate with frosted redcurrants.

3
ROOTS AND BULBS WITH HERBAL PROPERTIES

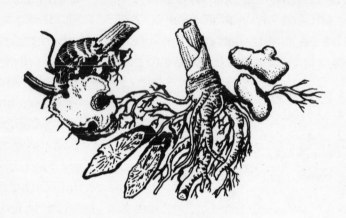

The subject of herbal roots is an area ripe for rediscovery. Among forgotten roots we can find earthy flavours, exotic cosmetics and Biblical aromatics. Like other solid fragrant substances, aromatic roots hold their perfume for years because the odorous molecules evaporate more slowly than in a liquid. This factor made them particularly valuable to ancient civilizations.

As meat became more affordable very few of the edible wild roots made their way into the vegetable gardens and so herbal roots for the cooking pot lost their popularity. In the seventeenth century, there were theories about the windiness, brain damage, melancholy and various negative states caused by eating roots. In his 1636 herbal, *The Historie of Plants,* Gerard writes of turnips which flower in the same year they are sown: 'they are a degenerat kind . . . causing frensie and giddinesse of the brain for a season.'

Roots made a culinary comeback in 1699, however, when the charming *Acetaria: A Discourse of Sallet* was published by John Evelyn. This book is an adventure in salad-making with instructions for gathering and preparing over 72 herbal roots, stalks, leaves, buds, flowers and fruits. Roots were boiled, sliced and tossed in oil and vinegar, some were boiled in wine, some pickled and others served with a white sauce. Evelyn includes treatment for the roots of beet, carrot, daisy, dandelion, garlic, goat's beard, mallow, onion, parsnips, parsley, radish, rampion, roccombo, salsify, scorzonera, sweet cicely and turnip.

One native root herb not mentioned by John Evelyn and no longer used is the early purple orchid (*Orchis mascula*). It was eaten in difficult times but also used in fertility rites because its double ovoid shape resembles testicles. Indeed the botanic name is from the Greek 'orkhis' meaning testicle. Sadly, this orchid is now rare and we may lose its unusual properties. Richard Mabey points out in *Food For Free* that it would be criminal to dig up any of the dwindling colonies for food. This plant provides a lesson in the valuable potential that can disappear forever when even one plant species is lost. The tubers contain bassorine, a starchy material which is more nutritious than any other single plant product. One ounce of the root, raw or cooked, will sustain a man for a whole day. Its root, dried and powdered, was used to make a thick nourishing drink called salop.

A similar nourishing drink is still served in China. It is made from powdered lotus root which creates a thick, white gelatinous 'drink', served warm and eaten with a spoon. It is very soothing for upset stomachs and occasionally available at tea houses for visitors suffering from travel sickness. It has little taste and up to a decade ago was flavoured with osmanthus flowers though now sadly it is more likely to be flavoured with something synthetic.

Aromatic roots have strong legendary links. Elecampane (*Inula helenium*) is named after Helen of Troy who was said to have been gathering this herb when she was abducted, and spikenard was used by Mary Magdalene to annoint the feet of Jesus.

Today, a herb garden can include many fine roots and bulbs such as: Welsh onion, everlasting onion, garlic, rocambole, wild garlic, marsh mallow, angelica, horseradish, roseroot, elecampane, soapwort, parsley, aniseed, skirret, sweet cicely, scozerona, salsify, lily root, galingale, chicory, dandelion, sea holly (*Eryngo root*), rosemadder, and dong-kwai (*Chinese angelica*). Ginseng needs crisp frost and snow in winter to create a good root so perhaps in the colder parts of Scotland a worthwhile root could be grown.

HARVESTING AND PRESERVING ROOTS

It is a root's function as a storage organ which mankind has found most useful. The nutritional content of the old pot herbs: carrots, turnips, parsnips, skirret, and the flavouring bulbs of onion and garlic are valuable because of the stored principles. Many of these principles have medicinal uses like those of valerian and ginseng. Others are aromatic like sweet flag, orris and rose root. Some are powerful spices like ginger, turmeric and galangal. There are many underground treasures just waiting to be mined.

Perhaps the main resistance to the use of roots is that it appears to end a plant's life by taking the root. But many of these roots, like horseradish and elecampane, spread and it is easy to dig a section of a root for culinary use, and benefit the plant by the pruning. Additionally, any thick piece of root like horseradish, comfrey or marsh mallow left in the ground will grow new shoots.

Roots are usually dug in the autumn when the goodness from the foliage has returned to the root for winter storage or in warm, but early, spring when root circulation is stirring but before it sends goodness back up the stems. When digging a piece of root with the intent of leaving the main part behind so that the plant will continue to grow, sever the piece neatly either with the sharp edge of a spade or a gardener's knife, depending on the size of the root.

Shake or gently rub off as much soil as possible. Then remove fibrous root hairs and scrub to clean. The value of some roots, such as valerian, is in their peel so in general this is not removed, though the roots of marsh mallow and the rhizomes of liquorice are peeled before being dried.

Drying Roots

Cut thick pieces of root lengthwise and then into slices to speed the drying process. Roots need a higher temperature than leaves to dry – about 120°F–150°F (50–60°C) – so they can be dried in a slow oven, turned frequently until they are fragile and break easily.

When completely dry, store the roots in airtight containers. They will keep for many seasons although the aromatic principles will slowly evaporate. Parsley and angelica root won't last for long, however, as they are hygroscopic, meaning they reabsorb moisture from the air. When they become soft they should be discarded.

Preparing Roots for Use

For an infusion, or decoction, pieces of any convenient size can be used; just bear in mind that the smaller the pieces, the more quickly will the desired principles be extracted to permeate the liquid. When purchasing dried roots, they are usually sold either powdered or in small, pea-sized pieces, very occasionally whole. Fresh ginger is the main exception and its soft texture is easy to grate and slice. For recipes requiring a powder they can be broken up as much as possible in a plastic bag with a rolling pin or hammer and can then be ground with a pestle and mortar. Very small amounts can be powdered in a domestic electric grinder but I have ruined one motor in an attempt to powder enough rhubarb root to use as a hair lightener.

CONTAINER HERBS

A collection of well-grown herbs in pots is a satisfying vision because experience teaches that the daily attention they require in summer indicates an orderly gardener with civilized priorities. To nurture herbs in pots is a labour of love with the extra bonus of convenient fresh herbs – chives for cream cheese before it melts on a baked potato;

mint as a sudden inspiration for a blackcurrant tart, or chamomile for a relaxing nightcap.

As most herbs are easy to grow in pots, town dwellers with only a balcony, roof garden or window box can enjoy the delights of a herb garden either outdoors or indoors. Supplying suitable conditions for roots is a main consideration for container herb growers.

Make sure your container has drainage holes and over these place gravel or broken crocks of terracotta. Terracotta is traditionally used because the shards have a little curve so they cover a drainage hole and still keep a little oxygen space, and because terracotta absorbs moisture storing a little extra for the soil mixture. Put a thin layer of grit or fine gravel and a sprinkling of horticultural charcoal granules (if available) over the terracotta. They help keep the soil sweet for herbs which have reached their largest size pot. Then use a good moisture retentive soil mixture.

There are good peat-based mixtures available from garden centres usually with a 'wetting agent' in them. This makes it easier to water the pots when they dry out, but my preference is still for a soil-based mixture. Peat becomes very light when it dries out and pots can be blown over in strong winds. Also, while sterilized soil has all the weed seeds and disease spores steamed out theoretically making it better, to me it feels dusty and lifeless. There is something about a home made mixture (7 parts loam, 3 parts peat, 2 parts sand plus fertilizer) made with a good rich compost, and lots of oxygen incorporated as you mix it like a giant Christmas cake in the wheelbarrow, that is worth putting up with the extra weeding. The herbs themselves discourage many of the diseases so I take my chances with live soil.

The size and condition of the roots of a herb determine when a pot-grown plant needs moving. Seedlings should be moved after they have grown four leaves – that is, their first two 'seed' leaves and two true leaves. By then their root system should be able to stand the shock of moving. Basil plants (like the tomato plants they are so delicious with), benefit from growing in shallow containers because the plant delays making leaf growth while the root is first growing down. The sooner the root hits a base, the earlier its leaves grow.

When you see the roots protruding through the base of a pot, that is the time to move it on to a pot one size larger. Try to use the same soil mixture as before and loosen the edges of the existing clump to help the roots blend into the new soil. Spring is the best time to re-pot as new roots grow most quickly. Avoid late autumn or winter because when the temperature drops below 47°F (7°C) no new roots will grow to anchor the plant.

The mobility of smaller containers gives you the opportunity to change their locations when it pleases you: place culinary herbs at the kitchen window; scented herbs near your favourite seat, and savoury herbs beside the barbecue. You can move them around to catch the sun or avoid the wind and they can be rearranged to enjoy their individual moments of glory. Allow them to migrate indoors for the winter or for one evening to the table so that guests can pick their own fresh garnish. They are also easy to monitor, to see what attention they need, but the flipside is that they require more attention than herbs in the open ground.

Herbs in pots need watering daily in hot weather – sometimes even twice because their roots have nowhere to extend in their search for extra moisture. Larger leaves like basil, lemon balm and sorrel appreciate a mist spray at mid-day in addition to their daily watering on hot days.

If you pick your herbs, try not to take more than one-third of the volume, though the herb will likely survive if even two-thirds is taken. Cropping herbs and the constant watering required by pots leaches the minerals from the pot and so frequent feeding is important for a healthy plant. Use a comfrey or nettle brew every two weeks in peak growing season.

Herbs for the Window Box

Choosing the culinary plants for a small window box is a challenge if you are used to the luxury of a herb garden. First, I think of the herbs I most frequently use fresh and could never be without – parsley and chives. Realistically, if you needed a lot for one recipe (like Tabouleh which takes a cup of chopped parsley) you would have to buy a batch, but for the odd, last-minute garnish and sprinkle I would want a fresh plant. Then I would select a lemon thyme, rosemary and sage which can each be kept small and tidy by judicial pruning. If I could keep the box warm in autumn I would include basil, otherwise I would keep it in a separate pot indoors. In a separate container I would also have a good flavoured spearmint such as Moroccan mint or Red Raripila mint. Allow at least 4 x 4 in (10 x 10 cm) for each herb and feed them every two weeks in spring and summer with a dilute liquid fertilizer if you are harvesting the herbs regularly. Try to choose an interesting range of leaf colour and size, such as silver thyme, purple basil and gold sage as there are several forms available of many of the common herbs.

With a larger window box, I could almost manage a herb garden. To the first six mentioned above I would add French tarragon, coriander, marjoram and treat myself to a lemon verbena. And I would tuck in a calendula or nasturtium for salad flowers to cheer me up.

Although a little unusual, lady's mantle in a hanging basket can be quite spectacular. The leaves invite inspection: beautiful green-pleated circles with a glistening crystal dewdrop in each centre. When the delicate pale yellow clusters of tiny flowers outgrow their slender stems they fall gracefully outward in a lacy crinoline around the basket.

COSMETIC USES

Carrots (*Daucus carota* ssp.)

Carrot root pulp appears to have several beneficial attributes for skin care. Dermatologists agree that the most important step for preventing wrinkles is to stop the sun's ultra-violet rays from reaching the skin. Creams with plant material that screens UV light are an important step. Aloe vera leaf gel is the most significant and it appears that carrot root may also contain significant amounts of a sun screening element. A cosmetic company reports that the difficulty has been for laboratories to combine the sun screen material with the other ingredients of a lotion as the sun screen materials either discolour or fail to emulsify.

Now, however, they have managed to blend carrot into a moisturizing skin cream and have also produced a macerated carrot oil which can be used as the oil component of your skin lotion recipes.

Carrots contain carotene (provitamin A), which is important for healing, B Vitamin complex, little Vitamin C, potassium salts, and it has antiseptic qualities. In the past it was used as a poultice to treat skin ulcers and cancerous sores and a carrot diet is still taken internally in some European treatment centres to alleviate the pain of cancer. But carrot juice must not be consumed in excess as it induces hypervitaminosis A. The pulp can be used as a face mask to help clear blemishes and to soften rough patches, leaving the skin silky smooth.

To make a face mask, steam roots until soft, cool, mash and stir in 3 drops of wheatgerm oil. Mix with Fuller's earth to create a paste (approx 1 tbsp [15 ml] Fuller's earth to ¼ cup carrot pulp), apply to the face and leave on for 15–30 minutes, resting with your feet higher than your head if possible. Rinse off with tepid water. Pulped marsh mallow root can also be used for its softening and soothing qualities.

Dandelion (*Taraxacum officinale*)

Dandelion is a blood purifier and taken internally to help clear eruptions, sometimes for eczema and to help remove calcium deposits from joints, a problem which can manifest on older hands. A wine glass-full of the decoction is taken twice a day. Externally, it is used along with horseradish root as an effective tonic wash or lotion to clear skin blemishes. The milky juice of the root and stems is said to remove warts. Roots are lifted in late summer, cleaned, then simmered in water for 20 minutes.

Horseradish (*Armoracia rusticana*)

The sliced root of horseradish boiled in milk and applied as a lotion will help clear spots and pimples. Lift roots in the autumn as the plant dies back, chop and decoct in milk or put through a juice extractor.

Madonna Lily (*Lilium candidum*)

The bulb of Madonna lily contains a great deal of mucilage which is soothing and softening to skin and it also has astringent properties. An ointment made from the juice of the bulbs has been used to remove inflammation from blemishes and heal the skin, including scars. The herbalist Gerard says 'It bringeth the hairs again upon places which have been burned or scalded, if it be mingled with oil or grease.'

Madonna lily has a reputation as being an effective antiwrinkle pomade which was very popular in Victorian times. Marsh mallow root shares this reputation. Lift bulbs in the autumn for cosmetic use.

To make a lily and marsh mallow rich face cream:

Lily, marsh mallow and carrot are all noted for antiwrinkle properties
1 oz (25 g) marsh mallow root
2 fl oz (50 ml) carrot oil
1 fl oz (25 ml) avocado oil
1 fl oz (25 ml) wheatgerm oil
1 lily bulb

1 oz (25 g) beeswax or anhydrous lanolin or a mixture
of the two
Beeswax makes the cream stiffer and shinier, lanolin softer
½ oz (15 g) clear honey
6 drops tincture of myrrh (for healing and keeping
qualities)

Crush the marsh mallow root. Blend the three oils together and macerate the marsh mallow root in this for two
weeks in a sunny window, stirring daily. Strain off the oils.
Put the lily bulb through a juice extractor to obtain about
1 fl oz (25 ml) of liquid.

Melt the wax or lanolin very gently in a double boiler.
Remove from heat and add the warmed infused oils slowly drop by drop, stirring the mixture constantly. Slowly
add the lily juice, beating constantly at first, then stir slowly until cooled to blood heat. Stir in the tincture of myrrh.
Spoon it into a wide-necked, sterilized jar, label and date.

A strong decoction of the lily and marsh mallow root
making 1 fl oz (25 ml) in total can be used instead of
macerating the oils and juicing the lily bulb.

Marsh Mallow (*Althaea officinalis*)

All the mallow family contains mucilage, a gummy substance which is emollient. This means it is soothing and
softening to irritated or inflamed surfaces so it is used
internally to smooth inflamed passages in chest complaints and externally on irritated skins, even to soothe
inflamed eyes. Marsh mallow has the highest percentage
of mucilage in the family and its root can yield half its
weight in mucilage. Collect in August and September

from plants at least two years old.

Marsh mallow roots do not yield all their desirable principles to boiling water so in many recipes they are soaked in cold water or boiled in wine or oil.

To make a marsh mallow infusion for rough skin: soak crushed root pieces in cold water for 8 hours, then strain and use the liquid. This infusion of mallow can be applied as a compress for rough and chapped hands, dry skin, dry hair and sunburn.

Orris (*Iris florentina*)

The fragrant rhizome of orris is dried and ground down for talcum powder. Three to four-year-old plants are lifted in the autumn, dried and kept for two years during which time their fragrance increases, before being distilled for essential oil. Orris root dry shampoo can be made as follows:

2 tbsp (30 ml) finely powdered orris root
2 tbsp (30 ml) powdered arrowroot or white Fuller's earth

Mix powders together. Part the hair in narrow strips and sprinkle the powder along each row until the whole scalp is covered. Massage lightly with fingertips to encourage absorption. Leave on for 10 minutes to absorb maximum grease and then brush out vigorously and thoroughly until the hair is shiny.

Potato (*Solanum tuberosum*)

The flesh of the common potato has a softening and slight

bleaching action on the skin. Peel and wash a freshly-dug potato and slice thinly. Rub several pieces on the face, leave for 30 minutes and wash off.

Rhubarb (*Rheum palmatum* or *R. officinale*)

The dried root is the strongest, natural, hair-blonding agent. The effect is accumulative and the colour becomes softer and deeper gold with each application. Drying the hair in the sun intensifies the lightening action, giving a rich, Titian, golden colour. A golden hair dye is made as follows:

4 tbsp (60 ml) finely chopped rhubarb root
1½ pts (900 ml) water

Prepare a strong decoction by simmering root in water for 20 minutes. Then allow to steep for several hours. This can be used as a rinse, catching the liquid and repeating the rinse action until the colour fades from the liquid. A more effective dye is achieved by making a paste. Add ½ cup kaolin powder (or Fuller's earth) to 1 cup of the decoction. Add 1 tsp (5 ml) of cider vinegar to maintain the hair's acid mantle and 1 tsp (5 ml) glycerine to prevent hair becoming dry. Wear gloves as rhubarb root stains and apply paste evenly throughout the hair. Leave on up to an hour and rinse well or let it dry on the hair and brush out later.

Sweet Flag (*Acorus calamus*)

Calamine lotion is a product of this rhizome; it is frequently dried and ground to create a scented talcum powder. It is also an ingredient of Chypre, the famous French perfume. Roots are lifted in the autumn, cleaned and distilled or dried in a low oven and ground.

HOUSEHOLD USES

Agrimony (*Agrimony eupatoria*)

The root and leaves of this common, wayside herb have a faint but pleasant fruity scent like green apple peel. This can be added to pot pourri and sweet bags.

Angelica Root (*Angelica archangelica*)

'To Perfume a House, and Purify the Air' (from *The Toilet of Flora* [1775]), take a root of angelica, dry it in an oven, or before the fire, then bruise it well and infuse it for four or five days in white wine vinegar. When you use it, lay it upon a brick made red hot, and repeat the operation several times.

Elecampane (*Inula helenium*)

When first lifted, the roots of elecampane smell of ripe bananas but as the root dries it acquires a camphorish, violet scent. Burn elecampane root over embers to scent a room or add shavings to pot pourri and sweet bags.

Ginger Family (*Hedychium species*)

This is a family of herbaceous plants from India that is among the most beautiful and sweetly scented in the world. It is mainly the flowers which radiate such exquisite perfume as to make them almost sacred but several of their roots are also beautifully scented.

Hedychium gardnerianum root supplies a product called Kapur-Kadri which is used in Eastern perfumery, and *Hedychium spicatum* root is dried and used as incense in Hindu worship. It has a strong, sweet, violet/orris scent. Its name is from the Greek for 'sweet snow' because of the white perfumed flowers. The extracted oil resembles the perfume of hyacinths.

Herbal Glue

A strong paper glue can be collected from home grown bluebell bulbs (*Endymion nonscriptus*) by scraping the side with a knife. This produces a thick sticky slime to be used straight away.

Indian Violet Grass (*Andropogon muricatus*)

The root of this herb has a violet perfume used by Eastern women. Another member of the family, *Adropogon nardus,* now reclassified as *Cymbopogon nardus* is highly aromatic in all its parts. The strongly-scented root smells of spikenard (hence the name nardus) and the leaves are the source of oil of citronella, a useful insect repellent.

Orris Root (*Calamus acorus*)

The lovely smell of sweet violets emanates from this dried root and it is the preferred fixative for pot pourris.

Rose Root (*Sedum roseas* or *S. rhodiola*)

The root of this herb is mildly scented of roses when dried. In Elizabethan times it was dried, powdered and soaked, or distilled to create a 'poor man's rose water' to sprinkle over clothes. From historic descriptions it seems the scent from the root used to be stronger, or perhaps a more scented strain was allowed to die out, but the scent in present-day roots is very faint.

Soapwort (*Saponaria officinalis*)

The cleaning service of an exclusive London company uses a medieval product on rare fabrics. The secret is soapwort, a cottage flower whose leaves and stems, but mainly roots, produce a detergent-free soap which does a remarkable job of cleaning ancient fabrics. Old skills were redeveloped at the National Trust's Uppark House, West Sussex, by the late Lady Meade-Fetherstonhaugh who found that soapwort not only removes dirt but revitalizes the texture, renewing the depth and brilliance of dyes. These skills are now being introduced to manor houses and museums worldwide.

Boil bruised root, leaves and stems of soapwort for ½-hour in a small amount of rain, soft water or filtered water, enough to keep the herb covered. Strain and use to wash, condition and revive delicate old fabrics, tapestries, silks and lace. Soapwort contains saponins which lubricate natural fabrics and absorb dirt, leaving fabrics with a softness and sheen.

Spikenard (*Valeriana jatamansi*)

This herb has a long history as a valued aromatic and was at one time the most costly fragrance available. The root has a strong, sweet, patchouli-like perfume and is the spikenard of the Bible. It was one of the ingredients in the ointment used by Mary Magdalene to wipe the feet of

Jesus whereupon the disciples rebuked her for using such a costly substance. The main reason for its expense was that it only grew in a few remote Himalayan valleys and the transportation problems by camel train through various climates and countries down to the Middle East were enormous.

It is a member of the valerian family and grows easily in Britain if you can find a source of the plant. Dry pieces to add to pot pourri or lay among clothes to perfume them.

Wood Avens or Herb Bennet (*Geum urbanum*)

The root of this herb has a clove-like scent which it retains when dried. Place dried root pieces in the linen cupboard or drawers to scent the clothes.

GARDEN USES

Inca Marigold (*Tagetes minuta*)

An important area of research where plants can be used to help or hinder the growth of their neighbours is in the study of root secretions. It seems that some trees pass messages in this way. If a host of caterpillars invades one birch tree, the chemical make-up of the plant changes, triggering its neighbours to produce a poison in their leaves that will repel the invaders. Some of the answers to companion planting may be found in this research which is long overdue.

The scent of Tagetes, the French or African marigolds, deters some insect pests and the root secretions have a powerful effect against eelworm. Dutch bulb growers plant it to protect their tulip crops and rose growers to protect roses. The common French and African marigold have some effect against the non-cyst forming eelworm (nematodes) but the most damaging eelworms are clustered 90–500 in cysts or shells which are impervious to chemicals. The most powerful tagetes is *Tagetes minuta,* the Inca marigold which can control these and enabled the Incas to grow potato crops on the same land for hundreds of years, free from the potato eelworm. This is an 8-ft (2½-m) plant (named 'minuta' after the tiny flowers) whose root secretions inhibit the eelworm's ability to sense the correct time to attack the potatos; they 'oversleep' and miss their host plant's appropriate stage.

The root secretions of *Tagetes minuta* have other remarkable effects: they can kill ground elder (*Aegopodium podagraria*), have a strong effect against bindweed (*Calystegia sepium*) and, to a lesser degree, against couch grass (*Agropyron repens*) in a circle around the herb. In Britain, the herb must be started early under glass as this tagetes needs a long growing season. Cut back the weeds in the area to be cleared to give the tagetes a chance to get ahead. When tagetes seedlings are 6-in (15-cm) tall, plant out at 12-in (30-cm) intervals over the area where weeds are to be eliminated. Allow to grow until frost kills them. Seed is available from the Henry Doubleday Association.

Garlic (*Allium sativum*)

Garlic and, to a lesser extent, the entire onion tribe are reported to repel aphids and seem to work in my greenhouse. However, it is not known whether it is the scent of the plants or a root secretion which creates a difference in the plant normally chosen by the aphids; perhaps both. The difference is significant because if it is the scent, then it is wise to plant the garlic near the greenhouse door to deter flying visitors but if it is the root secretions then it is important to plant the cloves near the plant requiring protection. If garlic does increase the scent of roses, as is claimed for this herb, it would make sense of the theory that root secretions of garlic trigger an increased essential oil production in roses.

WESTERN MEDICINAL ROOTS AND BULBS

Dandelion (*Taraxacum officinale*)

This common weed appears in Arabian herbals of the eleventh century and is still a useful herbal treatment. The root provides one of the safest plant diuretics known (a substance which increases the volume of urine), particularily valuable as it replaces the phosphorus usually lost with increased urination. Juice extracted from the root is used to stimulate the production of bile and a root decoction is drunk as a liver tonic especially for jaundice and the early stages of cirrhosis. It gives some benefit to sufferers of rheumatism and is taken as a mild laxative for chronic constipation. This herb is safe to take in fairly large amounts.

Garlic (*Allium sativum*)

Garlic has an ancient reputation as a herb for maintaining health and increasing stamina. This reaches back to records of the daily dose given to Egyptian pyramid builders and early Greek Olympic contenders. Present-day research confirms the historical claims made for this bulb and is discovering new virtues. It has strong antibacterial properties so it gives some protection against infectious diseases such as the common cold, amoeboid dysentery and even typhoid. Garlic lowers blood pressure and is used to treat hypertension and arteriosclerosis. It helps expel fluid from the lungs and is used to treat bronchial catarrh while the fresh juice was once employed as an inhalant for pulmonary tuberculosis. It is mildly fungicide and appears to fight the fungus which causes a fatal form of meningitis and the fungus of athletes' foot. It may also have a role to play in keeping tumours at bay. Unfortunately, the best way to reap the benefits is to eat a fresh clove once or twice a day. Garlic tablets generally have so little actual garlic in them that an enormous number is required to equal a clove. Taken in cooked dishes, garlic will provide most of the benefits so roasted cloves are a good idea. Chew fresh parsley or cardamom seeds at the end of a garlic meal to reduce the tell-tale breath.

Liquorice (*Glycyrrhiza glaba*)

The medical use of this plant stretches back 3000 years to the Assyrians, Egyptians and Chinese. The best roots are at least three years old and they are carefully dug up in late autumn, scrubbed clean and dried. The *British Pharmacopoeia* states that the root must be peeled but other authorities disagree. Liquorice has laxative properties and is used in the relief of Addison's disease but its primary value is in the treatment of coughs, bronchitis and gastric ulcers because of four main attributes. Liquorice root is expectorant – it helps expel phlegm; it is demulcent –

smooth and soothing to painful or inflamed areas; it is anti-inflammatory – it relieves inflamed surfaces; and spasmolytic – it relieves pain from spasms. In excessive doses liquorice may cause sodium retention and loss of potassium with resulting water retention, headaches, hypertension and shortness of breath.

Valerian (*Valeriana officinalis*)

The rhizome and roots of two-year-old valerian plants are a powerful nervine, a substance that calms nervous tension. Roots are lifted in September or October, washed and dried. Valerian root is not peeled because an important part of the medical properties resides in the skin. An infusion is made by soaking 1 tsp (5 ml) dried root in cold water for a day, and is drunk for nervous exhaustion, depression, anxiety, headaches, intestinal cramp and chronic insomnia. It is used in combination with other herbs to treat hypertension. Homoeopathic treatment uses a tincture of the fresh root. During the First World War, valerian was used to treat shell shock and, through the Second World War, to help people cope with the stress of constant bomb raids. Valerian should not be taken in addition to other sedative products and it is important to see a medical herbalist for an appropriate dosage. Do not take valerian in strong doses for long periods of time as it can become addictive.

CULINARY ROOTS AND BULBS

Garlic (*Allium sativum*)

The garlic bulb is universally an important seasoning. In its botanic name 'allium' is the name of the onion family and 'sativus' means 'sown, planted, cultivated' – hence also 'crocus sativus', saffron, the cultivated crocus. The bulb is made up of several corms, usually between 8 and 12, and their size and flavour varies with different climates and varieties, the best coming from warm climates.

Garlic is mainly used as a flavouring, but it can be roasted in the oven alongside any meat dish to create a delicious vegetable with a subtle flavour that does not have the pungency normally associated with the bulb. Garlic enhances all meats and fish and blends with most vegetables and herbs, particularly with parsley and mush-rooms.

Ginger (Zingiber officinale)

Ginger is the warmly-aromatic rhizome of a shade-loving perennial from the tropical jungles of south-east Asia. It has an ancient history as both a culinary herb and a medi-cine and was perhaps the first spice introduced to the West, long before the Roman empire was expanding. The plant has iris-like leaves and occasionally a flowering stem of white or yellow fragrant sterile flowers with a purple lip. The knobbly, buff rhizome grows like a stubby collection of fingers and at about ten months old it is collected and sometimes sold as a 'band'.

Ginger used to be only available as a powder which was popular in jams (like rhubarb and ginger jam); cakes such as parkin, and biscuits such as gingerbread men and ginger beer, but now the fresh rhizome is available in many supermarkets. It is only when using a plump, fresh 'root' that its true flavour can be appreciated validating its use as the primary spice for savoury dishes in oriental cooking. They use it with all types of meat, and also fish as it helps to transform the unpleasant fishiness of some species.

To use fresh ginger, first peel off the skin. If it will be used to flavour the cooking oil of a stir-fried dish, and then removed before main ingredients are added, it can be quickly sliced. But if it will remain part of the dish, grate it with the finest grade of a hand grater until it is almost like a paste. When buying ginger, choose pieces that have a tight, fresh, unwrinkled skin and store them in a cool, airy vegetable rack. Ginger maintains its life for long periods, so if you use it infrequently it will keep fresh if you plant it in a box of dry sandy soil and water it infrequently; sunlight is not necessary. It may even supply you with fresh green shoots which are the material of crystallized ginger.

Turmeric (*Curcuma longa*)

Turmeric is the fragrant rhizome of a tender perennial from south-east Asia with large lily-like leaves and dense clusters of pale yellow flowers. The rhizome, dug up when about nine months old, has intensely yellow flesh and is washed, boiled, sun-dried and has its skin peeled or rubbed off before being sold as a flavouring. It is usually only available as a powder but this is quite satisfactory as it is a tough root, very hard to pulverize at home, and it is a cheap enough spice so that middlemen are not tempted to adulterate it. It has a mild, 'dry', savoury flavour with a touch of bitterness and is in the same family as ginger. Its presence is mostly noted by the intense yellow colour it gives to curries, piccalilli and some Indian sweet dishes.

Turmeric is also used to dye monks' robes when saffron is too expensive, but it is not colour-fast. It should never be used as a saffron substitute in cooking as its flavour is too pronounced; calendula petals would be better just to supply the colour. In India, it is valued as an antiseptic and in hot climates this attribute gives extra protection to pre-pared food.

Horseradish (*Armoracia rusticana*)

The perennial root of horseradish grows wild in Britain in patches of moist ground. Locally it can often be found in the short drainage ditches dug out from the minor roads where the land lies low. Horseradish is a member of the mustard (cruciferae) family with dark-green, wavy-edged leaves up to 2 ft (60 cm) long and an occasional flower stem with pointed leaves quite different to the main leaves. The tap root is yellow ochre on the outside with a pungent white flesh. This flesh contains calcium, sodium, magnesium, Vitamin C and antibiotic qualities which make it useful for preserving food and protecting the intestinal tract. This is why it is often served with raw fish dishes by the Japanese as raw fish can contain parasites which survive in the human gut.

The root is prepared by scrubbing and then grating it, an experience never forgotten. The grating releases a powerful volatile oil which rushes up the nostrils and can clear sinuses in one breath. Most of the pungency is in the outer part of the root so peeling would mean the loss of most of the flavour. Only remove damaged or discoloured skin. The root can be grated with a fine grater or scraped off with a knife. Because the pungent oil evaporates so quickly there is little point in adding it to cooked dishes as the flavour will vanish during the cooking process. It can, however, be preserved by immersing the whole root in white wine vinegar.

TRADITIONAL ENGLISH HORSERADISH SAUCE
    2 tbsp (30 ml) finely grated horseradish
    1 tbsp (15 ml) white wine vinegar or lemon juice
    2 tsp (10 ml) castor sugar
    ¼ tsp (1.25 ml) made-up mustard
    salt and pepper to taste
    ¼ pt (150 ml) cream

Mix all the ingredients together except the cream. Half whip the cream and gradually fold in the horseradish mixture. Chill in the refrigerator until semi-solid and serve cold.

CREAMED HORSERADISH
On the continent, horseradish sauce is generally a lighter sauce made with cream and a little seasoning but without the vinegar of an English mixture.

    1 tbsp (15 ml) finely grated horseradish
    ¼ pt (150 ml) thick cream
    dash of lemon juice
    salt
    few drops olive oil

Gently stir the horseradish into the cream. Add the salt

and lemon juice. Beat in the olive oil drop by drop as an emulsifier to keep the mixture thick and smooth.

This is particularly tasty blended with cream cheese, garlic and chives to spread on canapés with smoked fish.

PICKLED HORSERADISH

Pick good sized roots, wash and scrape off any discoloured skin. Mince in a food processor or grate and pack loosely into small jars. Cover with salted vinegar (1 tsp [5 ml] salt to ½ pt [300 ml] vinegar) and seal.

The vinegar from this pickle can also be used as horseradish vinegar if the salt is acceptable to the recipe.

Liquorice (Glycyrrhiza glabra)

The dried rhizomes and roots of this hardy perennial herb of the pea family have the characteristic and popular flavour of the sweets named after the plant.

This pretty legume with racemes of small pale-blue flowers, grows in a rich, moist, sandy loam and three- to five-year-old roots are harvested when they have reached an extensive size. The roots are sometimes chewed raw but more often used in powdered form or as an extract. To produce the extract, the rhizomes and roots are ground into pulp, boiled in water and the resulting extract is concentrated by evaporation.

Liquorice flavours sweets, beers, tobacco and snuff. It is also used as a refreshing medicinal tea.

Onion (Allium cepa)

The entire onion family is valuable for cooks. There are no known poisonous members of the family, though a few varieties are rather rank. The common onion *Allium cepa* has many forms from spring onions and small pickling onions to giant main crops. The tree onion, also called the Egyptian onion and the Canadian onion (*Allium cepa* Proliferum), is a very hardy form which is easy to grow, producing small, sharply-flavoured onions on the stem tips in mid and late summer for pickles or garnish.

Bunching Onions

Bunching onions available from herb nurseries in Britain include the everlasting onions (*Allium perutile*) and Welsh onions (*Allium fistulosum*). These form a cluster of small bulbs rather than a single bulb. The everlasting onion was named as such because a few bulbs can be pulled off the side of a cluster and the remainder will stay to clump up again, giving a continuous supply. The everlasting onion is 9–12 in (22–30 cm) high with dark blue-green leaves and does not flower (it can only be propagated by plant division). The Welsh onion (Welsh meaning 'foreign') is a similar, but larger, plant producing a white flower cluster and stronger-flavoured leaves. The young autumn shoots stay green throughout the winter to give a supply of fresh 'chives'. Cut in thin slices with scissors to give rings of green for an attractive garnish.

Cultivars of the bunching onions are the most important onions in the Orient. The base is used like a large spring onion and the stems are blanched (grown with light excluded to produce tender pale shoots) to create the onion greens referred to in Chinese recipes. Two-inch (5-cm) lengths of these blanched stems, briefly stir-fried, are often the garnish on take-away meat and rice dishes available from street vendors in China.

Rocambole (*Allium sativum*)

This is a mild form of garlic with a small bulb and a long stem. In a warm summer it produces an attractive head of pinky-mauve flowers which develop into a cluster of tiny bulblets. All parts can be used as garlic and the leaves have a gentle garlic flavour like Chinese chives.

Shallots (*Allium ascalonicum*)

These are popular in French cuisine for their distinctive flavour and blend well with herbs. They grow in clusters and yield a medium-sized bulb which is excellent for pickles.

Dandelion and Chicory Coffee Substitutes

The long, milky, tap root of a dandelion dug when two years old and chicory root dug in the autumn of its first year make acceptable substitutes for coffee, giving a similar but slightly more bitter flavour, free from caffeine. Scrub the roots well but do not peel. Cut the chicory into short pieces but leave the dandelion whole and, if possible, dry them in the sun. Roast in a low oven with the door ajar until they are brittle. Store in an airtight tin and when required give them ten minutes further roasting in a hot oven. Grind them in a coffee grinder and use as you would coffee.

Florence Fennel (*Foeniculum vulgare* 'Dulce')

Fennel bulb is the swollen base of the stalks of Florence Fennel (the Latin *dulcis* means sweet or pleasant), and it is also called sweet fennel or Finocchio. This 18-in (45-cm) high form of fennel is grown as an annual and prefers a light, fertile soil. The most common problem is its frequent tendency to bolt whenever a cold or dry spell occurs. 'Zefa Fino' is a relatively new variety which is less prone to bolting. The 'bulb' has a fresh, crunchy texture and a mild, sweet aniseed flavour. It is popular grated or sliced into salads and can be prepared as a baked vegetable.

Salsify (*Tragopogon porrifolius*)

This is a root herb which faded from popularity when meat became cheaper earlier this century. It is a biennial with pretty purple flowers which can be pickled for salads. The root has a strong, individual flavour giving rise to its alternative name of the oyster plant as the taste is reminiscent of sea fish. Peel the long pale roots and steam them. Serve with butter, lemon juice and seasoning. It keeps its flavour well served cold and it can be sliced into salads.

Scorzonera (*Scorzonera hispanica*)

This herb is very similar to salsify but the flowers are yellow, the root has a dark brown skin and the plant is perennial. Prepare as for salsify.

Marsh Mallow (*Aithea officinalis*)

Originally, marsh mallow was made from the root of this herb by boiling slices in sugar water to create a soothing sweet paste, but today's marsh mallows have only the sugar in common with the original recipe.

2 oz (50 g) dried powdered marsh mallow root
14 oz (400 g) castor sugar
1 tsp (5 ml) gum tragacanth (available from chemists)
or other edible binding mucilage
2½ tbsp (37.5 ml) orange flower water (approx)

Mix the marsh mallow root and sugar together. Stir the gum tragacanth into 2 tbsp (30 ml) of the orange flower water. Add the liquid to the powders and stir. Use just enough orange flower water to bind the mixture together to form little balls. Roll into shape and leave these to dry.

If you cannot get the tragacanth, try soaking the powdered marsh mallow in the orange flower water overnight to draw out the mucilage from the marsh mallow, then add sugar and roll into small balls or, if it is not sticky enough, make into flat cakes, cut into squares and leave to dry.

Elecampane (*Inula helenium*)
This root contains a sweet starchy substance called inulin. In the Middle Ages, apothecaries sold the crystallized root in flat, pink, sugary cakes (coloured with cochineal) which were sucked to relieve asthma and indigestion and to sweeten the breath.

Sea Holly (*Eryngium maritimum*) (Eryngo)
Eryngo root has been a popular flavouring root since Saxon times with its sweet taste and high concentration of mucilage. The root was used medicinally and to make toffee. It is harvested in spring or in the autumn after seeding when it can yield roots up to 6 ft (2 m) long.

Roots are washed, parboiled, peeled and either dried or candied. To candy, slice thinly, weigh the eryngo and add an equal weight of sugar. Boil until the sugar becomes syrup, then cool.

SALAD ROOTS

John Evelyn's *Discourse of Sallet* reminds us of many salad roots long forgotten. He suggests chervil roots which should be boiled and eaten cold: 'much commended for Aged Persons'. Sweet cicely was sometimes called chervil and as the annual chervil roots are so tiny it is likely he means sweet cicely root. And they are remarkably tasty. He reports that the young roots of daisy are frequently eaten by Spaniards and Italians from spring until June and that French country people eat the root of dandelion. The history lesson continues with 'and t'was with this homely Sallet the Good-Wife Hecate entertain'd Theseus.'

The 'sallet's' ingredients included garlic, though he adds 'to be sure, 'tis not for Ladies Palats, nor those who court them; a light touch is better supplied by the gentle roccombo'. He lists the roots of goat's beard (*Tragopogon pratensis*) and scorzonera to be stewed and dressed for salads. Goat's beard is the same family as salsify (*Tragopogon porrifolius*) which John Evelyn called viper-grass or salsifex and stated it was 'a very sweet and pleasant sallet; being laid to soak out the bitterness, then peel'd may be eaten raw, but best of all stew'd with Marrow, Spice, and Wine.' Marsh mallow root was boiled to soften it and then sliced and fried. He adds parsnip boiled, cooled and eaten with oil and vinegar and radish whole or sliced.

His highest praise was reserved for skirret; 'exceedingly nourishing, wholesome and delicate; of all the root kind, not subject to be windy and so valued by the Emperor Tiberius that he accepted them for tribute. This excellent root is seldom eaten raw; but being boil'd, stew'd, roasted under the Embers, bak'd in Pies, whole, sliced or in pulp, is very acceptable to all palates. Tis reported they were heretofore something bitter; See what Culture and Education effects!'

CHERVIL/SWEET GICELY ROOT
Clean and peel the root, cut into strips and boil in salted water until just tender. Drain. While still warm, mix with a well-flavoured vinaigrette. Turn onto a dish and arrange with groups of very finely sliced radishes, peeled shrimps and watercress. The hot radishes and watercress contrast beautifully with the more subtly flavoured roots and shellfish.

JERUSALEM ARTICHOKES
1 lb (450 g) prepared Jerusalem artichokes
1 small onion
1 tbsp (15 ml) vegetable oil
1 tbsp (15 ml) flour
1 garlic clove
small glass of medium-dry white wine
approx ½ pt (300 ml) of single cream
salt and fresh ground white pepper
knob of butter
chopped parsley (optional)

Jerusalem artichokes need patience to peel, but it is well worth the effort. As soon as they are peeled, drop them into cold water acidulated with a squeeze of lemon or vinegar to prevent them from discolouring. When everything has been prepared for cooking, drain them and dry gently in a cloth.

Chop onion very finely and fry gently in the oil using a shallow casserole or straight sided frying pan. Sprinkle on the flour and combine well with the onion and oil. Stir in the mashed garlic clove.

Pour in the white wine and stir until smoothly blended. Season the sauce well.

Now add the prepared artichokes and enough cream to cover them. Simmer on the lowest possible heat for about ½ hour. Turn the artichokes occasionally with a spoon, but take great care, for as they soften, they can break up easily.

Either dot with butter and brown under the grill before serving, or sprinkle liberally with chopped parsley.

4
ESSENTIAL OILS

Scent is the first clue to the presence of a plant essence, or essential oil as it is called after it has been extracted by distillation. The plant essence is a cocktail of organic compounds found in minute glands in various parts of plants. It contains the aromatic and therapeutic principles used for flavouring, healing and cosmetics. Plant essences are also used for aromatherapy, the ancient art which uses blended essential oils for both beauty and health. They are mainly applied with massage.

Aromas, fragrances and perfumes are the elusive, desirable, unseen qualities of a plant that have stirred the passions and purse strings of humans through the ages. We have greater access to more of these fragrant treasures now than kings and empresses of any time in history. Of some 400 aromatic plants processed for their oils, at least 50 of the most beautiful are reasonably easy to obtain, from frankincense and myrrh (gifts from the Queen of Sheba to King Solomon 3000 years ago and later presented to the infant Jesus by three Wise Men); to tea-tree *(Melaleuca alternifolia)*, a newly discovered oil with antiseptic properties 12 times greater than phenol, the traditional hospital antiseptic. We can create exotic perfumes and effective cosmetics, revive pot pourri, make antiseptic room sprays with real plant perfumes, have aromatic baths, create insect repellents, give relaxing massage treatments for slimming and skin rejuvenation, help prevent stretch marks and cellulite, and treat minor ailments, both physical and mental, with essential oils.

On a world trade basis, the largest quantities of essential oils are used by the food industry; for example, peppermint oil in sweets. Pharmaceutical companies are the second highest consumers using them for products like toothpaste and gargles, although both industries will use a synthetic substitute if they can obtain it cheaper. Third, the oils are vital to the perfume trade which uses synthetics for certain oils for cost reasons but recognizes that the best quality only comes from pure plant essences.

Many of the plants which are processed for their essential oils are grown in our herb gardens: angelica, aniseed, basil, coriander, caraway, clary, chamomile, fennel, hyssop, lavender, melissa (lemon balm), peppermint, rose geranium (pelargonium), rose, rosemary, sage, spearmint, sweet marjoram and thyme. They are also found in the trees growing nearby: in pine, juniper, thuja and eucalyptus.

GROWING PLANTS FOR ESSENTIAL OIL

Several factors can influence the quality and amount of essential oil in a plant. First, the species is important. 'Norfolk Lavender' constantly grows new hybrids and then measures the quantity and quality of the essential oil in each variety. For the purpose of harvesting, they must also consider the size and growth pattern of the plant, the average length and number of flower stalks and the time required to reach maturity.

When a particular species is chosen, the soil fertility, drainage and climate will also influence the quality of oil. This is why oils from certain countries, such as Bulgarian rose or English sage, are considered the best of their kind. There is also a growing conviction that any sprays, such as insecticides, used on the plants are leaving traces in the essential oils so more and more customers are asking for organically grown sources of herb oils.

AROMATHERAPY

The term 'aromatherapy' was coined by Gattefosse, a French Professor of Chemistry who revived the healing use of essential oils during the First World War. Madam Maury, a biochemist and keen student of Gattefosse, recognized the potential of essential oils for skin care and was interested in the possibility that the oils could delay the ageing process. It was she who developed the massage techniques and formulae now usually associated with aromatherapy.

In France, where the medical potency of oils is recognized, aromatherapists must also be doctors and it is properly considered a form of healing. In other countries, however, because of the uncertain legal position of complementary medicines, aromatherapy is sometimes listed as a beauty therapy. Such is the healing power of essential oils that even those who enter the field strictly for cosmetic reasons become aware of the greater potential of these vital plant substances.

One definition of aromatherapy is as a healing art which uses essential oils to promote health and beauty of the body and serenity of mind, recognizing that beauty is an aspect of a healthy body and a healthy mind. In this therapy, essential oils are applied in small doses in a carrier oil directly onto the skin with massage. The massage aids the passage of essential oil molecules in their gaseous state through the skin into the lymph system and hence throughout the body.

Aromatherapy works on two levels: first, the aroma is perceived and this has a subtle but beneficial effect on the mind or nervous system and the mood or emotions. Specific oils can be selected to refresh and revive or to relax and soothe. Second, the cosmetic and medicinal properties of the oils (tonic, antiseptic, antispasmodic, etc) work on the physical body. They penetrate the skin and take 20–70 minutes to enter the bloodstream.

The massage itself plays a large part both in relaxation and stress management and as a beauty therapy, improving skin circulation. The essential oils also improve skin quality. It seems that they have a strong influence on the interchange of tissue fluid. This encourages the growth of new cells, helps eliminate old cells more quickly and accelerates toxic elimination. In this way toxic deposits and tissue debris are prevented from infiltrating the connective tissues which maintain an improved tissue state, both in the muscle and the skin. It is difficult to achieve this by any other means.

The following oils have been tested for toxicity, skin irritation and sensitization and are safe, with certain listed reservations, for normal diluted massage applications. All oils are for external use only.

Basil (*Ocimum basilicum*) Avoid internal use as it has some oral toxicity. In moderation it is a tonic, uplifting, energizing and an anti-depressant; it has a clarifying effect on the brain and is good for overworked muscles.

Benzoin (*Styrax benzoin*) (called a resinoid rather than an essential oil). It is penetrating and warming, stimulates circulation and helps heal cracked and chapped skins but has borderline results on skin sensitization.

Bergamot (*Citrus bergamia*) Hazardous on skin sensitization, bergamot has a fresh uplifting scent enjoyed by both men and women and is one of the most important anti-depressants. It is used in pot pourri and sweet bags. It increases the skin's sensitivity to sunlight making it tan faster (this is why it was previously used in sun creams) but this also leads to phototoxicity (a burn on the skin) and is implied in skin cancer. Use only in low percentages (the perfume industry recommends ½–1 per cent) and never apply before going into the sun. In the warm summer of 1989, several cases of bergamot burn were reported. Bitter orange, lemon and lime have similar photosensitizing properties. Bergamot is used to treat depression and anxiety.

Cajuput (*Melaleuca leucadendron*) Tested as safe, though practitioners say it irritates sensitive skins and it should never be allowed to come in contact with the mucous membranes. This is a penetrating camphorous medicinal oil which combats infections. Use it as an inhalant for colds and other respiratory infections but not before bedtime as it is a powerful stimulant. For most of its uses, its cousin niaouli (*Melaleuca viridiflora*), which is non-irritant, can be used instead.

Camphor (White) (*Cinnamomum camphora*) Safe, but brown and yellow camphor with the same botanic name are hazardous for skin irritation. It is cooling and stimulating and used to treat depression, insomnia and shock. It is good for oily skins and acne. Apply in a cold compress to reduce the swelling of bruises and sprains. Use six drops in a bowl with enough cold water to soak a cloth of the size required, squeeze and apply.

Caraway (*Carum carvi*) Safe. This is a stimulant and carminative oil which helps expel intestinal gas and ease the accompanying abdominal pain. It can be used to treat several parasites including scabies and mange in dogs.

Cardamom (*Elettaria cardamomum*) Safe. The plant has many medicinal uses in Indian Vedic medicine and the oil is used in perfumes and incense and claimed as an aphrodisiac in India. It can be used as a refreshing invigorating bath.

Cedarwood (*Cedrus atlantica, Juniperus mexicana* and *J. virginianal*) Safe. This oil is a sedative, antiseptic and an insect repellent. It is used to treat anxiety and cystitis but some recommend that it should be avoided in pregnancy.

Chamomile (Roman – *Anthemis nobilis;* German – *Matricaria chamomilla*) Safe. These two oils are a relaxing, refreshing pain reliever for dull aches. They benefit all skin types, especially sensitive, delicate and dry skins and those prone to allergies. They are used to treat depression and insomnia and to assist digestive and menstrual problems. They are very safe and the first choice for treating children.

Citronella (*Cymbopogon nardus*) Borderline hazard on skin sensitization. This oil is used as an insect-repellent and to keep cats off pot plants. Commercially, it is used in the manufacture of soaps and household disinfectants.

Clary Sage (*Salvia sclarea*) Safe, though some recommend it should not be used during pregnancy. A warming, soothing, nerve tonic used to treat depression, stress and tension, insomnia, asthma and dry skins. It is a powerful muscle relaxant but it can induce intoxication or euphoria and should not be administered to anyone about to drive a vehicle or who is likely to take any alcohol within a few hours.

Coriander (*Coriandrum sativum*) Safe. This is a sweet-scented, uplifting oil used to treat nervous debility, to aid digestion and reduce rheumatic pain.

Cypress (*Cupressus sempervirens*) Safe. A relaxing, refreshing astringent which improves circulation and mature skin. It is used to treat influenza and muscular cramps, and as a bath oil for haemorrhoids and varicose veins. As a deodorant and astringent it is useful for foot baths.

Eucalyptus (*Eucalyptus globulus*) Safe. A stimulating, antiseptic, anti-viral, insect repellent. It is a decongestant and used to treat cold, viruses and respiratory problems. It is an excellent oil to add to a humidifier in the autumn or a room spray. It also helps the formation of skin tissue and is used on cuts, wounds and burns. Eucalyptus oil will remove beach tar from clothes and skin.

Fennel (Sweet—*Foeniculum vulgare* 'dulce') Safe. Fennel is an anti-toxic oil and has been used to treat alcoholics by counter-balancing alcoholic poisoning. It may help prevent the build-up of toxic wastes in joints of the body which precedes inflammation. It is also used to treat cellulitis by French doctors. Fennel is a diuretic and for this it must only be used by medically trained personnel. It contains a precursor of a female hormone and has a role to play in regulating periods, treating painful periods and in the menopause. Fennel oil should not be given to epileptics or children under six.

Fennel (Bitter—*Foeniculum vulgare*) Hazardous on skin sensitization.

Frankincense (*Boswellia thurifera*) Safe. This oil is a warming, relaxing tonic and considered rejuvenating. It is used for respiratory problems as one of the best pulmonary antiseptics, for inflammation and wounds, and for improving mature skins.

Galbanum (*Ferula galbaniflua*) Safe. This oil is mainly used in the perfume industry and not often available to the public. It has the potential for use in treating skin infections and inflammations which are slow to heal.

Geranium (*Pelargonium graveolens*) 'Algerian' and 'Moroc' forms are safe; from 'Reunion' the oil tested as a borderline hazard on skin sensitization. This is a popular oil in aromatherapy which balances the production of sebum, and normalizes and cleanses all skin types. It is antiseptic and an anti-depressant, a refreshing, relaxing astringent and an insect repellent. It also assists hormonal balance and is used to relieve pre-menstrual tension. It stimulates the lymph system so it is useful in cellulite massage and to treat fluid retention.

Hyssop (*Hyssopus officinalis*) Borderline toxicity. Sedative and decongestant. It is used with caution to treat anxiety, hypertension, digestive and respiratory problems. It 'thins out' heavy catarrh so it is easier to expel and is used to normalize circulation. Applied in a cold compress, it is excellent for clearing bruises and has been used for those who have had a facelift. Never give this oil to anyone who suffers from epilepsy.

Jasmine (*Jasminum officinale*) Safe. A relaxing, seductive oil, highly valued in the perfume industry. It is used to treat depression, respiratory problems, uterine pain and is a tonic for sensitive skins.

Juniper (*Juniperus communis*) Safe. It is stimulating, anti-septic, astringent, diuretic and very useful for detoxifying the body in any condition where the toxins should be eliminated. It purifies and tones the urinogenital tract and is used to treat complaints related to this area, especially cystitis. It has a powerful ability to reduce urine retention, though if used in large amounts it will have the opposite effect. It is a good astringent bath oil for treating haemor-rhoids and it is used to treat aching muscles and respiratory problems. Juniper is useful for treating several skin conditions: acne, eczema, skin sores and possibly psoriasis. Many also use it for emotional, mental and physic cleansing; therapists and healers put a drop on each wrist to protect themselves from taking on ' negative' energy.

Lavender (*Lavendula angustifolium, L. hybrida* and *L. latifolia*) Safe. An oil with the widest range of applications because it is a normalizing herb. It is sedative, soothing, an anti-depressant, antibiotic, antiseptic, decongestant, an insect repellent and relieves sharp pain. This oil benefits all skin types and aids cell renewal. It is used to treat muscular pains, headaches, infections and colds, indigestion, poor circulation and insomnia. Lavender oil has been used to treat serious burns and war injuries. Two or three drops in a bath will help calm fractious children.

Lemon (*Citrus limonum*) Hazardous on skin sensitization. Lemon is refreshing, invigorating, antiseptic and an insect repellent. It is used to treat respiratory problems and sore throats. It is useful for oily skins, broken capillaries and as a minor bleach in skin care. It stimulates the production of white blood cells which help fight infections and is a powerful bactericide for treating wounds. A 2 per cent solution in water helps to stop bleeding of cuts. Lemon is a tonic to the circulation system and can be used neat to carefully treat a verruca, wart or corn. Apply 1 drop daily taking care to avoid the surrounding skin. Never use more than 1 per cent in a blend because of its possible irritating effect on some skins.

Lemongrass (*Cymbopogon citratus*) Safe. This is a strong tonic and powerful revitalizing antiseptic stimulant with deodorant properties. All the lemon scented herbs have insect repellent properties and this is no exception. It is useful for treating acne and oily skin though it is better to keep the percentage low as even though it has been tested as safe, some practitioners feel it may cause skin irritation. It is popular for improving circulation and muscle tone and valuable for massaging post-diet saggy skin.

Marjoram Sweet (*Marjorana hortensis* and *Origanum marjorana*) Safe. A calming and warming oil which is used in steam inhalations to treat bronchitis and colds. It has strong sedative properties and is used for several stress-related conditions like insomnia, tension, high blood pressure, headaches and muscular cramp. Do not confuse with origanum, or oregano (*Origanum vulgare*) which tested hazardous on skin irritation.

Melissa (Lemon balm—*Melissa officinalis*) No test results available. However, its lemon scent indicates that it should be used in low percentages (1 per cent) in blends in case of skin irritation, and although very popular with aromatherapists, who have used it for decades, they recommend caution as certain blondes and those with fair skins may experience skin irritation. As a bath oil, do not use more than four drops. It is refreshing and an anti-depressant, and calming and soothing. It is used to treat tension, neuralgia, digestion, fevers, painful menstruation, and respiratory problems. It is particularly good for the elderly.

Myrrh (*Commiphora myrrha*) Borderline hazard on toxicity. Myrrh is a tonic that is antiseptic, anti-inflammatory and healing. It is used to treat digestion, loss of appetite, catarrh, bronchitis and skin inflammations.

Neroli (*Citrus aurantium*) Safe. A beautifully scented oil, it is ambrosial, anti-depressant, antiseptic, anti-spasmodic,

146

an aphrodisiac and a sedative. It relieves anxiety, insomnia and emotional problems. It is famous in skin care for stimulating new cells, rejuvenating all skin types and especially for treating dry, sensitive skin.

Niaouli (*Melaleuca viridiflora*) No tests available but considered by practitioners to be tolerated by the skin and mucous membranes and can therefore be used as a gargle (always diluted) and vaginal douche. French doctors use it as an antiseptic in obstetrics and gynaecology. It is safer than its cousin cajuput. It is an antiseptic and disinfectant, and is soothing. The antiseptic and healing qualities resulting from its property of stimulating tissue growth make it useful for treating minor cuts, burns and skin ulcers. It treats respiratory problems, sore throats, colds and is a useful second string for acne. Patricia Davis, an experienced aromatherapist, suggests in *Aromatherapy, an A–Z* that a little-known but valuable use of niaouli is to reduce the severity of radiation burns from cobalt radiation therapy for cancer. A thin layer applied before treatment gives some protection from the burns and has been shown to reduce the severity of the burns.

Nutmeg (*Myristica fragrans*) Safe. Nutmeg is stimulating to the circulation and the heart and though it has been tested as safe, like all the spice oils it must be used with caution. It is a useful warming and toning winter oil to build resistance to colds.

Orange Sweet (*Citrus sinensis*) Safe. This oil is mildy sedative, an anti-depressant and is anti-spasmodic. It can be varied with other sedatives to reduce insomnia. Bitter orange is hazardous on skin sensitization.

Patchouli (*Pogostemon patchouli*) Safe. This is an antiseptic oil which is uplifting and an anti-depressant in small doses and a sedative in larger doses. Its cell-regenerating properties make it excellent in skin care for dry and mature skins. It is also a fungicide and the two properties are useful in treating acne, athlete's foot, some skin allergies, eczemas and dandruff.

Pepper Black (*Piper nigrum*) Safe. This is a warming oil which brings the blood to the surface, stimulating circulation. It is used to treat coughs, colds, high temperatures and muscular aches and pains. It is also employed to treat disorders of the digestive tract.

Pettigrain (*Citrus aurantium*) Safe. This oil is from the same tree as neroli with whom it shares several uses though it is less sedative and much less expensive. It is a refreshing bath oil with deodorant properties and a pleasant perfume.

Rose (*Rosa damascena* and *R. centifolia*) Safe. Rose is considered a very feminine oil and is used to treat a range of sexual and menstrual problems. It is cleansing and regulating for the uterus and menstrual cycles. It is also a very powerful healer for emotional problems and assists postnatal depression, stress and sadness. Rose is excellent in skin care for all skin types, especially ageing or sensitive skins. It is a tonic and astringent and regular applications will reduce thread veins. It is also used to improve circulation, digestion and to treat headaches. It is safe to use on children.

Rosemary (*Rosmarinus officinalis*) Safe. This is a toning and invigorating herb that stimulates circulation and brings blood to the surface. It is used for muscular and rheumatic pains. It lifts fatigue and aids digestion and headaches and is used in a range of respiratory ailments. It is said to improve hair growth. It stimulates the brain which has given it its memory strengthening reputation. It should not be used in excess as large amounts may cause epileptic-like fits.

Rosewood (*Aniba rosaeodora*) Safe. This is a pleasant-scented oil for perfuming the home or cosmetics. It is a gentle tonic which fights bacteria and is a useful deodorizing addition to the bath.

Sage (*Salvia officinalis*) Borderline hazard on toxicity. Sage has a powerful, warming, penetrating effect on muscles but it is safer to use clary sage.

Sandalwood (*Santalum album*) Safe. This has long been used in perfumes and body creams and it is well known for its beneficial effect of softening dry skins. Being astringent and antiseptic it is also good for oily skins and acne. Sandalwood is a strong pulmonary antiseptic and a sedative for dry, irritating coughs and chronic bronchitis. It is also used to treat fatigue, diarrhoea and nausea as well as being a strong urinary tract antiseptic.

Spanish Sage (*Salvia lavandulaefolia*) Safe. Although this oil has been tested as safe it may be wiser to use clary sage.

Spearmint (*Mentha spicata*) Safe. Do not confuse spearmint with pennyroyal which has high toxicity. Spearmint oil is mainly used in the food and pharmaceutical industries.

Tangerine (*Citrus reticulata*) Safe. A gentle oil, antiseptic, refreshing and pleasant in massage. It is also an insect repellent.

Tea-Tree (*Melaleuca alternifolia*) Its skin sensitization effect is untested but it is safe on toxicity. However, there are practitioners' reports of sensitive skins reacting to this oil. Although new to essential oil lists, the plant has been used by aborigines in Australia for thousands of years. It is a powerful antiseptic, the strongest of the known oils, and kills bacteria, fungi and viruses. It stimulates the body's immune system to fight infections and is used for colds, 'flu, catarrh and sinusitis. It can be used to control *Candida albicans* and be used to build up the strength of those scheduled to have an operation. There is also the possibility that it will be useful to AIDS sufferers if it can strengthen their immune system.

Thyme (*Thymus vulgaris*) Borderline on toxicity, hazardous on skin irritation. This strong pulmonary disinfectant is a useful massage oil or inhalant for all respiratory infections, cough, colds and sore throats. It increases white blood cells and therefore helps fight infections. There are forms of thyme oil available from specialist suppliers which are much less toxic and therefore very useful oils.

Vetiver (*Vetiveria zizanoides*) Safe. This is a fragrant scent much enjoyed by men and useful in pot pourri blends and perfumes for a rich woody tone.

Violet Leaf (*Viola odorata*) Safe. Violet leaf is a very expensive oil, seldom seen. It has valuable, skin-healing properties and may have pain-killing qualities.

Ylang-Ylang (*Cananga odorata*) Borderline hazard for skin sensitization. This is a heavy, sweet scent that is sedative, antiseptic and an anti-depressant. It slows down over-rapid breathing and hence it is used to treat anxiety, frustration, shock, fear or great anger. It is used for insomnia and to regulate circulation. This is another oil suitable for both dry and oily skins because of its regulating effect on the production of sebum. Use ylang-ylang sparingly as too much can cause headaches or nausea.

PERFUMES

Essential oils form the basis of quality perfumes. Some, such as rose, sandalwood and jasmine have been used alone as perfumes and rose is used in 96 per cent of women's perfumes and 42 per cent of men's perfumes.

A 'nose' (a person highly skilled in recognizing and blending aromas) will sit at a scent 'organ' which displays hundreds of fragrances. She or he will select aromatic notes to blend into chords. To evaluate the 'note' of a fragrance, a few drops of oil are placed on a wand to evaporate. If the scent is not detectable after 24 hours it is considered a top note. These are the scents in a perfume that would be noticed first: they are stimulating and uplifting. Basil, bergamot, citrus oils, eucalyptus, peppermint, sage and thyme are top notes. If the oil aroma is still noticeable after 24 hours, but not after 60 hours, it is a middle note. Middle notes form the body and substance of a perfume and provide its dominant character. Chamomile, geranium, lavender, hyssop, fennel, melissa (lemon balm), pine and rosemary are middle notes.

Oils detectable after 60 hours (usually for 6 or 7 days) are the base notes. Base notes are the fixative of a perfume, giving its lasting quality and a different aroma when the top notes have evaporated. Base notes are mainly sedative and calming. Benzoin, camphor, frankincense, myrrh, sandalwood, jasmine, rose and the spices – cinnamon, cloves and ginger.

Perfumes require alcohol to preserve the scent. By definition, perfumes are 15–25 per cent essences in pure (ethol) alcohol. *Parfum de toilette* is 12–15 per cent essential oils blended with over 50 per cent alcohol and some distilled water.

MEDICAL USES OF ESSENTIAL OILS

Essential oils should never be taken internally except when administered by qualified practitioners as they are very powerful substances, even potentially fatal. Taken through the digestive system the oils can be changed considerably by the hydrochloric acid of the stomach. Applied through the skin, mainly with massage or baths, these problems are obviated because the digestive system is bypassed.

They can be used to treat a number of conditions, but a qualified practitioner must be consulted for serious complaints. These oils must never be used neat. When the blended oils are applied with therapeutic massage movements the power of penetration is greater. The time may be 20 to 70 minutes to pass into the skin and then into the bloodstream. Check the general list of essential oils to see where caution is needed.

As Air Purifiers and Antiseptics

A spray of essential oils can kill bacteria, fungi and viruses to varying degrees in the air. Research was undertaken by a Dr Chamberland in 1887 on the antiseptic powers of vapourized essential oils, particularly on the anthrax bacillus. He found antigenetic potency (the ability to combat the development of germs and kill them) in decreasing order in: lemon, thyme, orange, bergamot, juniper, clove, citronella, lavender, niaouli, peppermint, rosemary, sandalwood, eucalyptus, and Chinese anise. This list corresponds with the respective terpene strength contained in each. They were most powerful against meningococcus, staphylococcus, and the typhus bacillus. Diphtheric bacillus were more resistant and sadly the spores of anthrax bacillus were not affected at all.

A French researcher L. Cavel published findings in 1918 on the antispectic qualities of several essential oils. He worked with sewage cultures and meat stock cultured in septic tank water, a fertile combination for the multiplication of bacteria. He tested essential oils in direct contact (rather than sprayed) to discover their ability to incapacitate the bacteria, making them infertile. He measured the minimum dose required per 1000cc of this stock to make the bacteria infertile. His results showed thyme to be the strongest at 0.7 parts per 1000, then origanum at 1.0, and then in steps for sweet orange, lemongrass, Chinese cinnamon and rose, down to clove at 2.0; eucalyptus, peppermint, rose geranium, meadowsweet, Chinese anise, orris, and wild thyme at 4.0; anise, mustard, rosemary, cumin, neroli, birch and lavender at 5.0; melissa, ylang-ylang and juniper at 6.0; sweet fennel, garlic and lemon at 7.0; cajuput, sassafras and heliotrope at 8.0; and turpentine, parsley and violet at 9.0. At the same conditions, phenol made the solution infertile at 5.6 parts per 1000.

Within this information, certain oils work more quickly against specific bacteria. For example, micro-organisms of yellow fever were easily killed by sandalwood and lavender oil. In a further test of the action of essential oils, bacteria usually encountered in the air were exposed to the emanations from essential oils for various periods. The results indicate that many of the bacteria were killed in less than an hour and in some cases after only a few minutes.

More research is required for a precise application. But it can be seen that a great many bacteria will be eliminated by spraying a combination of any of these oils into the air. Room sprays can purify the air of sick rooms, hospitals or doctors' waiting rooms, hair salons, schools, domestic rooms and offer special benefits for those whose immune system is weakened.

Fill 2 fl oz (50 ml) atomiser with 1 fl oz (25 ml) of alcohol (vodka or isoproy). Add 65 drops of essential oil of bergamot, 25 drops of lemon, 25 drops of lavender, 15 drops of orange oil, 15 drops of thyme, 15 drops of clove, 10 drops of juniper, 10 drops of tea-tree, 5 drops of peppermint, 5 drops of rosemary, 5 drops of sandalwood and 5 drops of eucalyptus. (Any combination will be effective.) Top up with distilled water and spray as required.

For Sport and Exercise Routines

Essential oils with massage are said to increase muscular and nervous tone, raise the general body resistance and make possible greater mental and physical effort.

For over-exertion, athletic stiffness or cramp from physical effort – lavender, marjoram, rosemary (to increase circulation), clary sage (sage is most penetrating for developed muscles but has toxic principles; use with caution and for men only). For organic cramp use geranium.

Not for Use

Do not use in pregnancy: pennyroyal is the most dangerous, sage and oregano next; basil, hyssop, juniper, myrrh, fennel, rosemary and clary sage, should be avoided until more is known about their actions.

Do not use for a person with skin sensitivity: thyme, basil, lemon, lemongrass, peppermint, tea-tree, pine.

Do not use in epilepsy: fennel, hyssop, sage.

INDEX